Meek
A N D
Lowly

NEAL A. MAXWELL

Meek

AND

Lowly

Deseret Book Company
Salt Lake City, Utah

This is not an official publication of the Church.
The author, and he alone, is responsible for the content.

First printing in hardbound edition, February 1987
First printing in paperbound edition, September 1994

Library of Congress Cataloging-in-Publication Data

Maxwell, Neal A.
  Meek and lowly.

  Bibliography: p.
  Includes index.
    1. Meekness—Biblical teaching. 2. Christian life—
Mormon authors. I. Title.
BS680.M39M39 1987   241'.4   86-32784
ISBN 0-87579-071-2 (hard)
ISBN 0-87579-945-0 (paper)

Printed in the United States of America

10   9   8   7   6   5   4   3   2   1

CONTENTS

ACKNOWLEDGMENTS

Deep gratitude is expressed to Daniel H. Ludlow, Roy W. Doxey, and Elizabeth Haglund, who read the manuscript in its early stages and made helpful suggestions. Most of all, they encouraged me.

Luke Ong kindly helped with some computer runs involving key words and key scriptures, which provided real assistance.

Susan Jackson patiently processed the manuscript through its several drafts.

My appreciation is also expressed to Eleanor Knowles of Deseret Book for the editorial suggestions that finally readied the manuscript for publication.

As always, my wife, Colleen, cooperatively yielded some July time so that this could be written.

Most of all, I am grateful to the prophets and writers of the holy scriptures for providing inspired words on meekness and lowliness, particularly in their portraying its full splendor in the life of our Savior. Indeed, when the Lord says, "My ways are higher than your ways," it is much more than methodology and style. His ways involve the supernal substance of transcending character—as this book, humbly, seeks to illustrate.

INTRODUCTION

Meekness ranks low on the mortal scale of things, yet high on God's: "For none is acceptable before God, save the meek and lowly in heart." (Moroni 7:44.) The rigorous requirements of Christian discipleship are clearly unattainable without meekness. In fact, meekness is needed in order to be spiritually successful, whether in matters of the intellect, in the management of power, in the dissolution of personal pride, or in coping with the challenges of daily life. Jesus, the carpenter—who, with Joseph, "undoubtedly had experience making yokes"[1]— gave us that marvelous metaphor: "Take my yoke upon you, and learn of me; for I am meek and lowly in heart." (Matthew 11:29.) The yoke of obedience to Him is far better than servitude to sin, but the demands are real.

Serious disciples are urged not only to do good, but also not to grow weary of doing good. (Galatians 6:9; Helaman 10:5.)

We are told to get on the straight and narrow path, but even when that is done, we are told that this is only the beginning, not the end. (2 Nephi 31:19-20.)

We are urged not only to speak the truth, but also to speak the truth in love. (Ephesians 4:15.)

We are urged not only to endure all things, but also to endure them well. (D&C 121:8.)

We are urged not only to be devoted to God's cause, but also to be prepared to sacrifice all things, giving, if necessary, the last full measure of devotion.[2]

We are not only to do things of worth, but also to focus especially on the weightier matters, the things of most worth. (Matthew 23:23.)

We are not only to endure enemies, but also to pray for them and to love them. (Matthew 5:44.)

We are urged not only to forgive, but also to forgive seventy times seven. (Matthew 18:22.)

We are not only to be engaged in a good cause, but we are also to be anxiously engaged. (D&C 58:27.)

We are not only to do right, but also to do right for the right reasons.

In the midst of all these things, we are given a day of rest, during which we do the sweetest but often hardest work of all.

Not only are we urged to worship God but, astoundingly, we are instructed to become like Him! (Matthew 5:48; 3 Nephi 12:48; 27:27.)

Who else but the truly meek could even consider such a stretching journey?

NOTES

1. *Interpreter's Dictionary of the Bible,* p. 925.
2. Joseph Smith, *Lectures on Faith,* lecture 6, no. 7.

Take my yoke upon you, and learn of me;
for I am meek and lowly in heart: and ye shall find
rest unto your souls. (Matthew 11:29)

Chapter One

TAKING HIS YOKE UPON US

"Take my yoke upon you, and learn of me; for I am meek and lowly in heart: and ye shall find rest unto your souls." (Matthew 11:29)

W hen we really learn of the Savior, it will be by taking His yoke upon us. Though this is a severe form of learning, there is no other way. When thus yoked, we get much more learning than we bargained for. Nor is His yoke to be removed partway down life's furrow, even after a good showing up to that point.

Did Jesus not say, "Take my yoke upon you, and learn of me; for I am meek and lowly in heart"? (Matthew 11:29.) Did Paul not speak of the "fellowship of [Christ's] sufferings"? (Philippians 3:10.) Are we not told that God gives us certain challenges and weaknesses in order to keep us humble? (Ether 12:27.) Did not Peter warn that disciples would know "fiery trials"? (1 Peter 4:12.) Meekness, therefore, is a major and necessary key to learning and improving, especially regarding the Lord, His plan, and our part in it.

Those who are meek sense, at least in part, what is actually underway even in the midst of this schooling. A highly matured Joseph Smith understood that he was passing through certain trials and afflictions that would one day permit him to be able to sit justified with ancient counterparts, such as Abraham, being thus qualified to hold an even weight in the balances with them.[1] We cannot come to know the full fellowship of Jesus' suffering without paying tuition of trial and experience.

When serious physicians plan their internships and residencies in medicine, they desire both sufficient quantity and sufficient complexity in the available clinical material from which they can learn. They often base their selection of learning sites upon the availability of clinical material in order to gain the appropriate learning experiences. As far as our mortal schooling is concerned, there is an abundance of "clinical material" all about each of us, more than we ever fully use. There is so much, in fact, that at times we may feel overwhelmed. We can maximize our mortal learning if, as we encounter the abundant experiences of life, we do so while striving always to be like Jesus, with His yoke firmly upon us.

Thus it is essential to resolve, early and firmly, what we think of Christ and whether we are really willing to take His yoke upon us. The insistent question— "What think ye of Christ?" (Matthew 22:42)—requires an answer, and if the answer is truly yes, we must take His yoke upon us.

The great back-to-back sermons of Alma and Amulek were given to a group who had been "taught...bountifully before [their] dissension." However, the group had also been told by false teachers, from time to time, that there would be no rescuing Christ. The concerned audience had inquired what they should do. Amulek spoke concerning "the coming of Christ," hoping to "plant the word" in their hearts, because "the word is in Christ unto salvation." Listeners were urged to "try the experiment of its goodness." Discerning Amulek then employed a rare and descriptive phrase: "The *great question* which is in your minds is whether the word be in the Son of God, or whether there shall be no Christ." (Alma 34:2–5. Italics added.)

This is still the "great question" for mortals. Anciently, it was whether there *shall be* an atoning Jesus Christ. Now it is whether there *was* an atoning Christ who lived and who still lives. Other questions are insignificant by comparison, since an affirmative answer to the "great question" eliminates the need even to ask certain lesser questions.

Once people can establish faith that Jesus was and is the Christ, a second and powerful "great question" naturally follows: "What must we do to become like Him and to join Him in the Father's kingdom?" Of this need for deep developmental commitment, the Prophet Joseph Smith declared that "the situation of the saints" is such that "unless they have an actual knowledge that the course they are pursuing is according to the will of God they will grow weary in their minds, and faint."[2]

Among the qualities to be developed in order to make that breathtaking journey, and to be more like Him and later with Him, is the quality of meekness. It is upon this quality that so many other things, in turn, depend. Without meekness, we cannot accept the gospel, be baptized worthily, maintain our faith, or enjoy the companionship of the Holy Ghost. Without meekness, we cannot retain a remission of our sins, nor can we come to have still further knowledge about Jesus Christ. And, finally, without meekness, we cannot enjoy the highest gospel ordinances worthily.

Yet neither meekness nor the other Christlike virtues—all of which are interactive and cross-developed—can be produced in an instant or in a vacuum. Instead, their development requires taking Jesus' yoke upon us in order to learn of Him through the blend of intellect and experience.

Nevertheless, it is ironical even to write of the virtue of meekness, especially in a world so much taken up with assertiveness, aggressiveness, and selfish, insensitive individualism. This virtue will seem anachronistic in the world, which, ironically, is failing for want of it whether in high political places or in marriages and families. Even so, as the world becomes more hard and more coarse, it remains for the true disciples of Jesus Christ to strive to become more like their meek Master. Otherwise one could pay only a modicum of attention to meekness and lowliness, duly noting them and rejoicing that at least such have been perfected in the Father and Son. It is not simply a matter of our having received mild encouragement to become meek and lowly. Rather, meekness is at the center of an astonishing invitation and commandment:

"Be ye therefore perfect, even as your Father which is in heaven is perfect." (Matthew 5:48.) "I would that ye should be perfect even as I, or your Father who is in heaven is perfect." (3 Nephi 12:48.) "Therefore, what manner of men ought ye to be? Verily I say unto you, even as I am." (3 Nephi 27:27.)

The relevance of meekness to daily life is unquestioned, for we clearly think and behave differently, depending upon whether we live with or without meekness.

Meekness is a facilitator in the development of all the other Christian virtues. Combined with the other virtues, it supplies many human needs, including perspective. After cataloging various qualities, such as faith, virtue, knowledge, temperance, patience, godliness, kindness, and charity, Peter declared that if an individual lacks these qualities, he will not be able to "see afar off." (2 Peter 1:5-9.) Determining whether we will live myopically and selfishly or live now for eternity is a fundamental decision that colors every day of daily life. To live a life of "thanksgiving daily" (Alma 34:38) while in the midst of adversity and its tutorials is impossible without a degree of meekness.

Furthermore, in the exchange between Jesus and a righteous young man, we can see how one missing quality cannot be fully compensated for by other qualities, however praiseworthy: "The young man saith unto him, All these things have I kept from my youth up: what lack I yet? Jesus said unto him, If thou wilt be perfect, go and sell that thou hast, and give to the poor, and thou shalt have treasure in heaven: and come and follow me. But when the young man heard that saying, he went away sorrowful: for he had great possessions." (Matthew 19:20-22.)

To be lacking in one quality or be casual about its serious development, as in the instance just noted, where the missing meekness prevented a submissive response, does alter one's perspective and vital decisions. Meek individuals will be aware of their need to develop each of these cardinal qualities; being meek, they will initiate a program to develop them and steadily pursue that development, especially those virtues that may be lacking. Meekness is thus essential for receiving counsel from Church leaders, lest, lacking such, we find ourselves on the fringe of the Church or even outside it. What the unmeek actually do is refuse to enter the realm of their own spiritual possibilities.

Whether we are giving and receiving feedback, growing intellectually in order to understand truths we "never had supposed," or remembering so that the Holy Ghost can preach to us from the pulpit of memory, the volume of blessings to flow therefrom is determined by our meekness.

Granted, meek individuals are apt to have periodic public relations problems, being misrepresented and misunderstood. They will have to "take it" at times. Even so, there appears to be no other way to achieve certain learning except through the relevant clinical experiences. "Take my yoke upon you, and learn of me; for I am meek and lowly in heart," Jesus said. Happily, the command-ment carries an accompanying and compensating promise: "and ye shall find rest unto your souls." (Matthew 11:29.) This special form of rest surely includes the shedding of certain needless burdens, such as fatiguing insincerity, exhausting hypocrisy, and the strength-sapping quest for praise and power.

Those of us who fail in one way or another almost always do so because we carry unnecessary and heavy baggage. Thus overloaded, we then feel sorry for ourselves. We need not carry such baggage, but when we are not meek, we resist the informing voice of conscience and feedback from leaders, family members, and friends. Whether from preoccupation or pride, the warning signals go unnoticed and unheeded. However, if we have sufficient meekness, we will have help to jettison unneeded burdens and keep from becoming mired in the ooze of self-pity. Furthermore, the metabolism of meekness requires very little praise or commendation, of which there is usually such a shortage anyway. Otherwise, the sponge of selfishness quickly soaks up everything in sight, including praise intended for others.

On the other hand, when they do not have sufficient meekness, individuals may engage in Church-bashing while at the same time being patted approvingly on the back by those who egg them on and yet fail to see the irony. Judas doubtless had his rationalizations, as when he told the priests and scribes, "Whomsoever I shall kiss, . . . lead him away safely." (Mark 14:44.) When individuals are too busy watching the applause meter, they fail to see what is happening to themselves. They miss as well what is happening to unsteady observers. Those who are lukewarm usually cool down the faith of others; the Church member who is half-informed and half-committed may quarter the faith of the weak. The adversary is quick to try to use any ambivalence or disobedience as a wedge between us and the Lord, as in his ancient attempt with Adam and Eve. (See Genesis 3:1–10.)

In our failures, there is usually disguised selfishness, the overreaching for "a bridge too far." Whether in financial or civic ruin or in infidelity and divorce, proud selfishness is usually there. Lack of intellectual humility is there among those who have deliberately cultivated their doubts in order, they think, to release themselves from their covenants. Some nurture their grievances assiduously. Were their grievances, instead, Alma's seed of faith, they would have long ago nourished a mighty tree of testimony.

Those who are not meek are often reluctant to give up a worn-out issue, complaining even after previous pain has stopped and harboring disappointments long after they are relevant. We simply cannot make for ourselves a "new heart" while nursing old grievances. Just as civil wars lend themselves to the passionate preservation of grievances, so civil wars within the soul do the same.

Christ consistently, demonstrably, and successfully resisted the ego considerations that we mortals have experienced altogether too often in ourselves and in others. He did so in premortality (Abraham 3:24–27) as well as in mortality. Had our Lord been a lesser being, He might have sought the reassuring reverberations of recognition or derived pleasure from succulent status, instead of joy from meek and lowly service regardless of the reproaches. Had Jesus been only half as meek and submissive, He might have still made a truly exceptional showing in mortality but still not have finished His great atoning work. Therefore, if our emulation of Him is to be serious, amid rampant egoism, we should ponder how, in the midst of all these things, He was so self-disciplined and meek.

To labor in the Lord's vineyard is lowly work, as the world measures comparative worth. No wonder, as one prophet wrote, the laborers in the Lord's vineyard are so comparatively few. Moreover, the work will not be performed in a luxuriant Eden, but often in "the poorest spot in all the land of [the] vineyard." (Jacob 5:21.)

In the great premortal council, when Jesus meekly volunteered, saying, "Here am I, send me" (Abraham 3:27), it was a most significant moment: a few words were preferred to many, for the meek do not multiply words. Never has one individual offered to do so much for so many with so few words as did Jesus when, having created this and other worlds, He then meekly proffered Himself as ransom for all of us on this planet, billions and billions of us!

By contrast, in our unnecessary multiplication of words, we often display a lack of clarity or betray an abundance of vanity. Our verbosity is sometimes a cover for either insincerity or uncertainty. With more subtraction of self, there would be so much less multiplication of words. Would we remember and use His Sermon on the Mount if it were thirty pages long?

Jesus' appreciation and His meekness are impressive at every turn. Of the Lord who directed the miracle of the loaves, John recorded, "There came other boats from Tiberias nigh unto the place where they did eat bread, after that the Lord had given thanks." (John 6:23.) Christ, the fashioner of the miracle of the loaves, actually and genuinely thanked His Father for the bread. It was a real prayer of gratitude, not simply pedagogy to teach His disciples how to pray. Christ, the Bread of Life, was thankful for some crusts of bread; He also had His followers gather up all that remained. Whether in attitude or in action, those of us guilty of the sin of ingratitude must strive more to be like Him. This, too, in the midst of both His tender and severe mercies. (1 Nephi 1:20; 8:8; Ether 6:12. See also Genesis 32:10; Alma 34:38; D&C 46:15.)

Jesus' townspeople were among the first mortals to witness another dimension of His kindness. They are recorded as marveling, early in His ministry, at His "gracious words"—not alone the unexpected fluency of the carpenter's son, but also His graciousness. Should it surprise us that it was so? For so it should be with us in our associations and conversations. Graciousness is a soothing and lubricating dimension of love; it is especially needed when the yoke is most heavy and chafing.

Is there not deep humility in the majestic Miracle Worker who acknowledged, "I can of my own self do nothing"? (John 5:30.) Jesus never misused or doubted His power, but He was never confused about its Source either. But we mortals, even when otherwise modest, often are willing to display our accumulated accomplishments as if we had done them all by ourselves. The Lord warned the Israelites about such arrogance: "Thou say in thine heart, My power and the might of mine hand hath gotten me this wealth. But thou shalt remember the Lord thy God: for it is he that giveth thee power to get wealth, that he may establish his covenant which he sware unto thy fathers, as it is this day." (Deuteronomy 8:17-18.)

Sometimes when there is accumulated arrogance, we leave the Lord no other remedy: "Yea, and we may see at the very time when he doth prosper his people, yea, in the increase of their fields, their flocks and their herds, and in gold, and in silver, and in all manner of precious things of every kind and art; sparing their lives, and delivering them out of the hands of their enemies; softening the hearts of their enemies that they should not declare wars against them; yea, and in fine, doing all things for the welfare and happiness of his people; yea, then is the time that they do harden their hearts, and do forget the Lord their God, and do trample under their feet the Holy One—yea, and this because of their ease, and their exceedingly great prosperity. And thus we see that except the Lord doth chasten his people with many afflictions, yea, except he doth visit them with death and with terror, and with famine and with all manner of pestilence, they will not remember him." (Helaman 12:2-3.)

How much of our mortality is spent unmeekly in

rearranging the furniture of our relationships and in the interminable organizational shufflings, usually because of ego rather than for any genuine increase in our effectiveness? How many new thrusts are simply new extrusions of old, untamed ego? There can even be a drunkenness of conscientiousness, if we are not anchored in meekness to help us to detect excessiveness in ourselves.

Instructive, indeed, is that circumstance in which the believing mother of James and John unmeekly pressed the Savior in behalf of her sons, hoping they might later sit on his right hand and on his left. Jesus did not indignantly reprove the worshipful and good mother. Rather, He spoke truthfully to her, saying she did not realize what she asked. He noted that this particular decision was His Father's anyway. Later that day, He further taught ten indignant apostles (and presumably James and John as well) about being servant-leaders.

The mother's petition resembled so many of our prayers. We do not realize the implications of what we ask. We ask amiss and then wonder why such petitions are not granted precisely as submitted. (3 Nephi 18:20; 2 Nephi 4:35; James 4:3.) Those who are meek experience, on occasion, not knowing what to "pray for as [they] ought." Instead they let the Spirit itself make intercession. (Romans 8:26.) "And it came to pass that when Jesus had thus prayed unto the Father, he came unto his disciples,... and they did not multiply many words, for it was given unto them what they should pray, and they were filled with desire." (3 Nephi 19:24.) "He that asketh in the Spirit asketh according to the will of God; wherefore it is done even as he asketh." (D&C 46:30.)

If, therefore, we truly want the best for our sons and daughters, we want for them not status but more meekness, mercy, love, patience, and submissiveness—the things that will rise with them in the resurrection, when so much else stays behind.

Several times, concern arose over precedence among the original Twelve—one time with some "strife." Jesus sought to disabuse His disciples about status in connection with His final Passover feast. Once more, He stressed to them their leader-servant role. (Luke 22:24–30.) Finally, having washed their feet, He pleaded with them to love one another, as He loved them. (John 13:34.) Likewise, the Nephite Twelve were carefully counseled against having doctrinal and other disputations among themselves. (3 Nephi 11:22, 28.)

Can we, in our quests for praise, status, power, and wealth, excuse our compromises because of the powerful and incessant temptations? It was Christ who displayed incredible integrity when the adversary made Him an offer that the adversary felt could not be refused—"all the kingdoms of the world, and the glory of them." (Matthew 4:8.) But He refused!

Christ's remaining possession, a cloak, was gambled for even as He died. (John 19:23–24.) Yet the very earth was the footstool of Him who was meek and lowly! Jesus gave mankind living water so that we shall never thirst again. In return, on the cross He was given vinegar.

Had Jesus not been meek and lowly when "a great multitude with swords and staves" came to take Him (Mark 14:43), He could have, in pride, resisted His destiny. Led by Judas, there came a band of men "thither with lanterns and torches." (John 18:3.) Spiritually blind, the multitude needed lanterns to see and to capture the "Light of the world."

Meekness makes sublime submissiveness possible, that submissiveness without which no real spiritual development would be possible. Righteous sorrow and suffering carve cavities in the soul that will become later reservoirs of joy. Moreover, the meek not only understand when such reservoirs are being readied, but also that those reservoirs often fill gradually. So, too, the gradual stretching of our frail spiritual muscles by stress can strengthen the very sinews necessary to exercise tough love. Such isometrics require patience and meekness.

It is so easy to focus on things temporal, neglecting the Master: "For how knoweth a man the master whom he has not served, and who is a stranger unto him, and is far from the thoughts and intents of his heart?" (Mosiah 5:13.)

Amulek said that though he was called many times, he "would not hear. He actually knew concerning these things, yet he would not know." (Alma 10:6.) He is a classic case of an essentially good man being out of touch with the great spiritual realities; he resisted the things of the Spirit because, though he was basically good, he was preoccupied with the cares of the world. When meekness was needed, it was sufficiently there in Amulek. As a result, he became yoked, and he then experienced the costs of discipleship, "having forsaken all his gold, and silver, and his precious things, which were in the land of Ammonihah, for the word of God, he [Amulek] being rejected by those who were once his friends and also by his father and his kindred." (Alma 15:16.)

Fortunately, God is preoccupied with His children. We (and what we may become) are His work and glory. (Moses 1:39.) All that He does is for our benefit. (2 Ne. 26:24.) As George MacDonald said of God, "He lays no plans irrespective of His children."[3] "Worlds and suns and planets," wrote MacDonald, are but "a portion of His workshops and tools for the bringing out of righteous men and women to fill His house of love."[4]

The meek are neither ashamed of Jesus Christ (2 Corinthians 7:14) nor embarrassed by His yoke, His gospel, and His ordinances. They proceed meekly with their lives within the framework of faith and rely upon the gospel's affirming answers to the "great question."

Prophets are included in this process of "yoked" development. Their shortcomings and imperfections are known, but the meek will see evidence of these merely as minor debris scattered along life's battlefield in the sacred struggle of prophets to deepen their discipleship and to become even more like the Master whom they serve.

Paul wrote of experiencing the "fellowship of Christ's sufferings" (Philippians 3:10), concerning which Paul was certainly no stranger. To the elders from Ephesus, he declared that he had served the Lord "with all humility of mind, and with many tears, and temptations, which befell [him] by the lying in wait of the Jews." (Acts 20:19.)

Likewise, Nephi was familiar with the "great goodness of the Lord." (2 Nephi 4:10-23.) After telling about the Lord's mercies to which he had been a witness, he asked: "O then, if I have seen so great things, if the Lord in his condescension unto the children of men hath visited men in so much mercy, why should my heart weep and my soul linger in the valley of sorrow, and my flesh waste away, and my strength slacken, because of mine afflictions? And why should I yield to sin, because of my flesh? Yea, why should I give way to temptations, that the evil one have place in my heart to destroy my peace and afflict my soul? Why am I angry because of mine enemy?" (2 Nephi 4:26-27.) As he concluded his record, Nephi declared unequivocally, "But I, Nephi, have written what I have written, and I esteem it as of great worth, and especially unto my people. For I pray continually for them by day, and mine eyes water my pillow by night, because of them; and I cry unto my God in faith, and I know that he will hear my cry." (2 Nephi 33:3.)

Several times the New Testament usage of the word "meek" or "meekness" is unsurprisingly tied directly to the Old Testament:

The meek shall inherit the earth. (Psalm 37:11.)	Blessed are the meek: for they shall inherit the earth. (Matthew 5:5.)

Rejoice greatly, O
daughter of Zion; shout, O
daughter of Jerusalem:
behold, thy King cometh
unto thee: he is just, and
having salvation; lowly,
and riding upon an ass, and
upon a colt the foal of an
ass. (Zechariah 9:9.)

Tell ye the daughter of
Sion, Behold, thy King
cometh unto thee, meek,
and sitting upon an ass,
and a colt the foal of an ass.
(Matthew 21:5.)

Being meek and lowly stresses the humility of the Sovereign. Our King is unconcerned with either the trappings of power or the assertion of His immense and incomparable prestige, for He "made himself of no reputation, and took upon him the form of a servant, and was made in the likeness of men." (Philippians 2:7.)

Jesus' willingness to become a person of "no reputation," though He was actually the Creator of this world—with the earth being His footstool—provides one of the great ironies in human history. This individual of "no reputation" mortally will one day be He before whom every knee will bow and whose name every tongue will confess. (Philippians 2:10-11.) He stayed the course!

Brigham Young, who stayed the course, knew the fatigue of leadership. He counseled those less secure about the outcome, "It is the Lord's work. I know enough to let the kingdom alone, and do my duty. It carries me, I do not carry the kingdom. I sail in the old ship Zion, and it bears me safely above the raging elements."[5] In our own time, the late Elder LeGrand Richards was heard by some of us to declare that he did not fret about the Church because it is the Lord's church: "I let *Him* worry about it!"

When we are meek and "settled" in our hearts (Luke 21:14), we know that the Lord watches over His church, filled as it is with imperfect leaders and people. To be sure, instructive feedback is needed at all levels, just as it is needed in healthy marriages and families. Information and inspiration are likewise needed at all levels. Having so said, it is the Lord's church, and those who are too eager to steady it and too quick to focus upon a single issue or concern will fail to comprehend the important undergirding function of meekness that includes trust in the Lord.

Anxious Uzzah, who steadied the ark in ancient Israel, was smitten for his actions. (2 Samuel 6:6; 1 Chronicles 13:9.) Some may reason that he was only trying—though mistakenly—to help out. But given the numerous times the Lord had saved and spared Israel, including the high dramas of the Red Sea and of the manna from heaven, surely He knew how to keep the ark in balance! Was Uzzah steadying the ark out of sincere but naive concern? Perhaps. But he would also have been carefully instructed as to his duties, which should have check-reigned his eagerness. Meekness is neither alarmist nor shoulder-shrugging unconcern. It involves shoulder-squaring self-discipline, and what follows is the special composure that meekness brings.

Besides, what Uzzah did could have become a pattern, at a time when there was already too much second guessing of Moses. What if a pattern had developed in the modern-day church wherein, like James Covill, the Saints could say, in effect, "I'll go, dear Lord, but I'll go where I want to go"? This lesson is an old one, as in Jonah's trying to go to Tarshish instead of Nineveh, to which he had been called.

At issue is our obedience to the Lord. Has he not said, "To obey is better than sacrifice, and to hearken than the fat of rams"? (1 Samuel 15:22.) Obedience is what is needed, because through obedience we can grow and become more like Him. Ancient Israel, blessed with the miracle of manna, went contrary to instructions, leaving it overnight against the fear that God would not provide on the morrow—and "it bred worms, and stank." (Exodus 16:20.) The Lord can provide for His people. The Yokemaster is able to do His work, and those of us yoked to His purpose must not forget that reality.

If we trust the Lord, perform our duties, and keep the commandments, the Lord—so far as the course of His Church is concerned—is able to do His work and to bring to pass that which has been planned from "the foundation of the world," back beyond time.

Whether our challenge involves our relationship to God, to His church, to His prophets, to our spouses or family members or neighbors, meekness is vital for our happiness and spiritual success. The stumbling blocks thereto are large and many, and none is larger than our management of our own roles, influence, and power, all of which Jesus managed perfectly.

NOTES

1. Dean C. Jessee, *The Personal Writings of Joseph Smith*, p. 395.
2. *Lectures on Faith*, lecture 6, no. 4. See also Hebrews 12:3.
3. George MacDonald, *Anthology*, p. 43.
4. MacDonald, p. 44.
5. *Journal of Discourses* 11:252.

Chapter Two

LEADING IN MEEKNESS

"We have learned by sad experience that ... almost all men, as soon as they get a little authority, ... will immediately begin to exercise unrighteous dominion." (D&C 121:39)

In few things is genuine meekness so essential as it is in the opportunities and responsibilities in connection with power. As we ponder the experiences of followership and leadership in the Church, certain lessons emerge. In one way or another, each of these lessons turns upon the meekness factor. If we in our leadership assignments take upon us the yoke of Jesus, we soon begin to learn of Jesus as a result of those leadership experiences. Appreciation of Christ then deepens into adoration.

Again and again, we see the difference between that genuine meekness which comes "because of the word" (Alma 32:14) and that temporary meekness which comes because of circumstances or events. Again and again, we see people who are happily "in a preparation to hear the word" (Alma 32:6), but also people who flourish for a brief season but then wither because they have no root. He whose gospel net it is told us that this would be so: "The kingdom of heaven is like unto a net, that was cast into the sea, and gathered of every kind." (Matthew 13:47.)

In taking the yoke of Jesus upon us, we learn of Him by coming to understand better His deep commitment to leadership through love and to free agency, amid the opportunities from which people have to choose, even if they choose evil and misery. We see, again and again, that except for the extreme discipline of excommunication and withdrawing fellowship from erring members, the

17

Church functions within the arena of agency, teaching correct principles, providing examples, and giving counsel. (D&C 134:10.) Furthermore, we have been expressly cautioned against seeking to exercise control, dominion, or compulsion in any unrighteous degree over others. Instead, we are to exhibit long-suffering, persuasion, gentleness, meekness, and love unfeigned. (D&C 121:37-41.) Emulating His style and substance of leadership quickly teaches us more about Him.

Surely such experiences acquaint us directly with the yoke of Jesus. Furthermore, we truly learn how meek and lowly was and is He who had access to ultimate power.

We see, again and again, how the trends of the world affect the human environment. The prophecy of Paul spells out some of the conditions of the last days: individuals would be lovers of themselves, covetous, proud, unthankful, unholy, and without natural affection. (2 Timothy 3:2-3.)

The Moffatt Translation of the Bible renders these words "selfish, fond of money, boastful, haughty, abusive, disobedient to their parents, ungrateful, irreverent, callous, relentless, scurrilous, dissolute, and savage; they will hate goodness ... [and] keep up a form of religion [but] they will have nothing to do with it as a force." (See also Romans 2:20; 2 Nephi 28:5; Joseph Smith-History 1:19.)

The pattern of having "a form of godliness, but [denying] the power thereof" (2 Timothy 3:5) is sometimes expressed in weak faith or in a commitment to a passive god. *Form* survives, but some will have nothing to do with religion as a *force*. Occasionally this occurs because partial believers are ashamed of their faith. Believers are sometimes the telling significance of certain scriptural adjectives chided by agnostics for following "some unknown being ... who never has been seen or known, who never was nor ever will be." (Alma 30:28.)

Paul was deeply concerned over those who had

begun to worship and serve the creature rather than the Creator. (Romans 1:28.) One of the expressions of indulgent self-love, which is the refusal to deny self, is the breaking of the seventh commandment whether by fornication, adultery, or homosexuality. As Jesus said, these and other signs are the foretelling leaves of the fig tree, indicating that "summer is nigh." (Matthew 24:32.)

The responsibilities of leadership in the Church include helping members to live in such a world without being overcome by it. In process of time, we will understand better, personally and experientially, why some are called but others chosen. Some of the "called" are not finally "chosen" because, unmeekly, (1) their hearts are set too much on the things of this world, (2) they aspire to the honors of men, and (3) they do not learn that the powers of heaven are accessed only through righteousness. Since the Lord's kingdom is to proceed in a system of long-suffering and persuasion, gentleness, meekness, and love unfeigned (it cannot really go forward otherwise), each of us has ample opportunity to develop patience and meekness.

As we take His yoke upon us, we come to appreciate the telling significance of certain scriptural adjectives and adverbs, such as "almost all" (D&C 121:39) and how people may "sometimes" be humble but only because of events and circumstances (Alma 32:13). Even Laman and Lemuel were humbled, though briefly, "because of the word"; otherwise their humility almost always required bracing events that, finally, did not bring about real change. (See 1 Nephi 15:20; 16:3.)

In developing a meek and lowly personality, the possession of power is both a great privilege and a terrible risk. However, of the risks and privileges of power, those who are meek not only learn more rapidly from the Spirit, presently and prospectively, but also from the lessons of the past. As Samuel Coleridge wrote: "The light which experience gives us is a lantern on the stern which shines only on the waves behind us."[1] Happily for us, the light of the gospel shines in all directions and at all times for those who have eyes to see. But the light of history, including secular history, playing upon the past, can provide important lessons for today and tomorrow.

In *The March of Folly*, historian Barbara Tuchman has written, "Chief among the forces affecting political folly is lust for power, named by Tacitus as 'the most flagrant of all the passions.' Because it can only be satisfied by power over others, government is its favorite field of exercise."[2] A few examples from power's "favorite field" follow.

Both secular and spiritual history remind us of how much we have been given by way of powerful, even stunning, insights in the lessons of the past. Without these insights, however, and without the meekness to take advantage of them, we will continue to witness human history as "the march of folly."

Meekness and humility are thus not only important for salvation, but also for society and government.

Barbara Tuchman has further observed how fortunate America was to have had as one of its Founding Fathers George Washington, who had such "a character of rock and a kind of nobility that he exerted a natural dominion over others, together with the inner strength and perseverance that enabled him to prevail over a flood of obstacles. He made possible both the physical victory of American independence and the survival of the fractious and tottering young republic in its beginning years."[3]

Those whom we describe as our Founding Fathers have been called by Arthur Schlesinger, Sr., "the most remarkable generation of public men in the history of the United States or perhaps of any other nation." Barbara Tuchman noted that "it would be invaluable if we could know what produced this burst of talent from a base of only two and a half million inhabitants."[5]

The Lord, if we are meek enough to listen to Him, has told us of the divine design associated with that "burst of talent": "For this purpose have I established the Constitution of this land, by the hands of wise men whom I raised up unto this very purpose, and redeemed the land by the shedding of blood." (D&C 101:80.)

The exercise of power requires an especially sharp and sensitive conscience, not a dull one. Therefore, meekness and humility are involved, without which both conscience and Spirit are constrained. So dulled, a person is not likely to listen to peers or to consider the lessons of history.

The capacity to lead is associated with the capacity to learn, vital at any age and in any role, lest there be what historian Tuchman calls "mental standstill or stagnation." Even so, she continues, "leaders in government... do not learn beyond the convictions they bring with them; these are 'the intellectual capital they will consume as long as they are in office.' Learning from experience is a faculty almost never practiced."[5]

In contrast, the Lord has counseled us directly, not obliquely, that we undergo certain experiences that can be for our good. (D&C, sections 121–122; Mosiah 23:22; Abraham 3:25.) But all this requires meekness so that the requisite learning can occur!

Besides, almost all persons do have difficulties managing power and status. (D&C 121:37.) One devoted public servant who ably served several British Prime Ministers as their private secretary observed: "Vanity is a failing common to Prime Ministers—...and I suppose it is natural in view of the adulation they receive but to which they are not, like Kings, accustomed."[6]

Winston Churchill displayed oratorical brilliance very early in his parliamentary career, but he also displayed some crudity in certain of his early speeches.[7] Churchill, by and large, learned to correct this insensitivity and insolence in his remarkable parliamentary career, which is a further tribute to him. It was on display in a 1905 episode in which Churchill attacked Prime Minister Balfour and his government. Churchill had badgered the government for some time, but this attack "drew blood." It involved a speech that some said was one of the most insolent ever heard in Parliament: "We have been told *ad nauseum* of the sacrifices which the Prime Minister makes.... I do not deny that there have been sacrifices. The house ought not to underrate nor deny those sacrifices. Some of them must be very galling to a proud man. There were first the sacrifices of leisure and then sacrifices of dignity.... Then there was the sacrifice of reputation.... It has been written that the right honorable Gentleman stands between pride and duty. Pride says 'go' but duty says 'stay.' The right honorable Gentleman always observes the maxim of a certain writer that whenever an Englishman takes or keeps anything he wants, it is always from a high sense of duty."[8]

Balfour had heard enough. "Unfolding his six feet to reply to the accumulated insults of months, his long-fingered hands clasping the satin lapels of his frock coat, he administered a lesson that Churchill would not forget":

> As for the junior member for Oldham, his speech was certainly not remarkable for good taste, and as I have always taken an interest in that honorable Gentleman's career, I should certainly, if I thought it in the least good, offer him some advice on that particular subject. But I take it that good taste is not a thing that can be acquired by industry, and that even advice of a most heartfelt and genuine description would entirely fail in effect if I were to offer it to him. But on another point I think I may give him some other advice which may be useful to him in the course of what I hope will be a long and distinguished career. It is not, on the whole, desirable to come down to this House with invective which is both prepared and violent. The House will tolerate, and very

rightly tolerate, almost anything within the rule of order which evidently springs from genuine indignation aroused by the collision of debate. But to come down with these prepared phrases is not usually successful, and at all events, I do not think it was very successful on the present occasion. If there is preparation, there should be more finish, and if there is so much violence, there should certainly be more veracity of feeling.[9]

Churchill later developed his capacity to be generous, including to the vanquished, even to those who had been recipients of political disgrace. This was seen in his tribute to Neville Chamberlain, whom he had earlier replaced as Prime Minister, showing how far Churchill had come from his brasher days. Churchill generously described how Neville Chamberlain "in one of the supreme crises of the world [was] contradicted by events": "History with its flickering lamp stumbles along the trail of the past, trying to reconstruct its scenes, to revive its echoes, and kindle with pale gleams the passion of former days.... The only guide to a man is his conscience; the only shield to his memory is the rectitude and sincerity of his actions.... With this shield, ... we march always in the ranks of honour."[10]

Another fascinating and instructive example comes from a more ancient realm. It too involves a setting of war, insurrection, and terrorism. There was an exchange of correspondence between Moroni, the chief captain of the armies, and Pahoran, who was chief judge and governor of the land in a time of great turmoil. (Alma 60–61.) Anxious Moroni did not have all the facts, as is evident in his biting complaint to Pahoran. Pahoran's meek reply is a lesson to us all, as it certainly must have been to Moroni.

Moroni wrote "by way of condemnation" seeking to know the cause of his army's sufferings for want of government support. He envisioned Pahoran and his colleagues as merely sitting upon their thrones "in a state of thoughtless stupor," doing too little to aid the army. Then came the unkindest cut of all: "We know not but what ye are also traitors to your country." Moroni then urged Pahoran and his colleagues to "bestir" themselves, or Moroni would come back and smite them with his sword.

The reply of Pahoran, as chief judge and governor, to his chief captain in the field begins, "Moroni, . . . I do not joy in your great afflictions . . . but . . . there are those who do." Pahoran advised that dissenters had mounted a successful insurrection against the government; this was the reason Moroni's armies did not have adequate provisions. In fact, Pahoran and his colleagues had actually been driven out of the city and had fled to the land of Gideon. Pahoran was at work rallying the people to him. Meek Pahoran then delivered this tender reproof: "And now, in your epistle you have censured me, but it mattereth not;[11] I am not angry, but do rejoice in the greatness of your heart. I, Pahoran, do not seek for power, save only to retain my judgment-seat that I may preserve the rights and the liberty of my people. My soul standeth fast in that liberty in the which God hath made us free." (Alma 61:9.)

Pahoran invited Moroni to join forces with him, concluding, "Now I close my epistle to my beloved brother, Moroni."

Pahoran's was not a resentful rejoinder lamenting the fact that Moroni was foolish without the facts. Pahoran did not engage in sarcasm or bitterness by lamenting that things were at least as rough for him as they were for Moroni and the army. He could have been sarcastic, saying he no longer had any throne to sit upon "in a state of thoughtless stupor." He could have justifiably boiled over at the accusation of his being a traitor, telling Moroni to do his job as chief captain and that Pahoran would do his job as governor. Instead, this exchange permitted these two leaders to rally themselves and their forces to retake the city. Moroni, when he received Pahoran's reply, indicated that his "heart did take courage," and that he rejoiced "because of the faithfulness of Pahoran." (Alma 62:1.)

Where individuals have said too much with too little data, meekness plays a very crucial, correcting role in what follows. Whether it is Pahoran reminding his general in the field so tellingly, or Prime Minister Balfour tutoring a prospective Prime Minister, Winston Churchill, in a way that "may be useful to him in the course of what...will be a long and distinguished career"— meekness proves crucial.

In contrast to the manner, style, and substance with which the Lord would have his power and authority used (as set forth in D&C 121), secular systems of power contain their own modes and alluring rewards. Disraeli, as Prime Minister of England, wrote that while some might talk of the "bore and bother of patronage and all that, the sense of power is delightful, it is amusing to receive the letters I do....I had no idea I was the object of so much esteem." He then realistically noted, however, that "as nobody in the world, were I to die tomorrow, would give up even a dinner party, one is sensible of the form of life."[12]

Even so, later when the time came for Disraeli—who had said, "I live for power and the affections"—to give up power for the last time, he described it as "the most painful passage in political life, the transition from power to obscurity....Winding up a Government is as hard a work as forming one without any of its excitement."[13]

The authority of example and considerations of character, unlike pudding, are not whipped up in an instant. This episode in the life of George Washington involving potential mutiny so illustrates:

Washington called together the grumbling officers on March 15, 1783. They filled the hall called the Temple, which served for worship, dances, and conferences. He began to speak—carefully and from a written manuscript, referring to the proposal of "either deserting our Country in the extremest hour of her distress, or turning our Arms against it...." Washington appealed simply and honestly for reason, restraint, patience, and duty—all the good and unexciting virtues.

And then Washington stumbled as he read. He squinted, paused, and out of his pocket he drew some new spectacles. "Gentlemen, you must pardon me," he said in apology. "I have grown gray in your service and now find myself growing blind."

Most of his men had never seen the general wear glasses. Yes, the men said to themselves, eight hard years. They recalled the ruddy, full-blooded planter of 1775; now they saw ... a big, good, fatherly man grown old. They wept, many of these warriors. And the Newburgh plot dissolved.[14]

An unmeek George Washington could have railed at these lesser military leaders, reminding them of his personal and financial sacrifices and describing what the war for independence had cost him. He could have harangued and threatened to quit. In a moment of near defeat, it was more than the tactic of a soft answer turning away wrath. Washington's whole character was placed on the line, and the tamed officers knew it.

The exemplar's eloquence may go unheeded, but it cannot be surpassed in its authenticity.

Washington's magnanimity was noteworthy even in victory. At the conclusion of the miraculous Constitutional Convention of 1787, he deliberately appointed some of those who had lost on certain issues to help draft the final document. He did so in order that the losers might see some of their words in the final document, the later ratification of which proved no less miraculous than its creation. Without a critical mass of wise leaders, the birth of the American nation would have been stillborn, and Washington's meekness was one key to his greatness.

There was a significant linkage between two great military and political men, the Duke of Wellington and George Washington: with all their greatness they both had considerable meekness and humility. Wellington observed on one occasion: "I have always felt the Highest respect for the character of General Washington."[15]

The Duke of Wellington had a refrain, "I am but a man," which is not unlike the story of Washington riding through a small town and overhearing a girl of seven who had been brought out to see him, the hero, exclaim, "Why, he is only a man!" whereupon General Washington swept off his hat, bowed, and said, "Yes, miss, that's all I am."[16]

Wellington, who was frequently plied with questions for years after his great victories, particularly the victory at Waterloo, reflected his humility even in his humor. Asked whether he'd had a particularly good view of the Battle of Waterloo, Wellington replied, "I generally like to see what I'm about." Another inquiry asked if he was "surprised at Waterloo." Wellington replied, "No, madam, but I am now!"[17]

Near the end of his life, the Duke was asked if he had one thing he would do differently, what that would be. Presumably the question concerned hindsight as to some military strategy in some great battle. The Duke surprised his listener by saying, "I should have given more praise."[18]

The interaction of great people and those who follow them is one of mutual trust and respect. Wellington, whose relationship with his troops was special, observed: "Besides, my army and I know one another exactly. We have a mutual confidence, and are never disappointed."[19]

Truly great individuals are not anxious to have themselves elevated. After all, even angelic emissaries from the Lord have bidden overwhelmed mortals to arise because they are fellow servants. John the Revelator said: "I fell at his feet to worship him. And he said unto me, See thou do it not: I am thy fellowservant, and of thy brethren that have the testimony of Jesus: worship God: for the testimony of Jesus is the spirit of prophecy." (Revelation 19:10. See also Revelation 22:9; 1 Nephi 17:5.)

The unrighteous use of power—not just familial or ecclesiastical, but all expressions of it—carries certain consequences: "he is left unto himself." (D&C 121:38.) This is not the loneliness of final responsibility felt in righteous leadership when decisions and actions devolve poignantly upon one's soul. Rather, unrighteous dominion brings an erring individual face to face with the echoing hollowness of soul.

The meek leader, having "humbleness of mind" (Colossians 3:12), is freer. He is relieved of the pressure to be the single or even the chief source of ideas for the group. Nor need he be the sole source of his group's memory. He lets others, too, report what they see by the light of "the lantern on the stern." He need not be afraid to praise, lest someone gain on him, for he follows the pattern of sharing and rejoicing in the achievements of others shown so effulgently by the Father and the Son. After all, the meek and lowly Leader did not need bands and banners: "Behold, thy King cometh unto thee, meek, and sitting upon...a colt." (Matthew 21:5.)

Just as the cream comes to the top when cold milk is left to sit awhile, so will the meek be generous in their memories, recognizing past blessings. They listen when the Holy Ghost preaches to them from the pulpit of memory, for they have "proved" the Lord "in days that are past."[20]

Meekness permits us to seek spiritual things by faith. Ancient Israel failed, said the Apostle Paul, for "they sought it not by faith." (Romans 9:32.) They preferred something else: "They despised the words of plainness, and killed the prophets, and sought for things that they could not understand. Wherefore, because of their blindness, which blindness came by looking beyond the mark, they must needs fall; for God hath taken away his plainness from them, and delivered unto them many things which they cannot understand, because they desired it." (Jacob 4:14.)

The humble leader sees the need to provide maintenance for the followers as well as help to get the tasks done. Though conscientious, he will sense, as did the Master, when respite and renewal are required. The need for such refreshing pauses occurs to the meek leader, for he remembers how, in the Lord's vineyard, the laborers are few and they often labor in "the poorest spot." (Jacob 5:21, 70.)

Should pride first protrude and finally prevail, whether in connection with the early stages of our understanding or in the final stages of our submitting, we are much at risk. After all, one should not expect to take his bows on the mortal stage just as the curtain opens.

Lucifer deeply desired to be "worshipped" in "act one" of our premortal life, as well as later. (Moses 1:19.) Thus, pride not only "goeth before...a fall" (Proverbs 16:18), but pride also precedes a failure to ascend, spiritually. Lucifer did not want the responsibilities of godhood. These include shepherding and truly loving a disobedient mortal flock who are possessed of free agency that will be misused, resulting in many not being saved and in many falling short of their possibilities. Leadership can call forth bossiness instead of meekness in a leader, if he is not careful. The agency of others can so easily be subordinated to the desire for smoothness and control. A believing and articulate British scientist, Alan Hayward, has written perceptively of God's style of leadership as compared to an illustrative episode:

Suppose for a moment that God made His presence felt all the time—that every action of ours, good or bad, brought an immediate response from Him in the form of reward or punishment. What sort of a world would this be then?

It would resemble, on a grander scale, the dining room of a hotel in Africa where I once stayed for a few days. The European owner evidently did not trust his African waiters. He would sit on a raised platform at one end of the room, constantly watching every movement. Goods that might possibly be pilfered, such as tea bags, sugar knobs and even pats of butter or margarine, were doled out by him in quantities just sufficient for the needs of the moment. He would scrutinize every bill like Sherlock Holmes looking for signs of foul play.

The results of all this supervision were painfully obvious. I have stayed in many hotels around the world, including a dozen or so in five African countries, but never have I met such an unpleasant bunch of waiters as in that hotel. Their master's total lack of trust in them had warped their personalities. As long as he was watching they acted discreetly, but the moment they thought his guard was down they would seize the opportunity to misbehave.

In much the same way, it would ruin our own characters if God's presence were as obvious as that of the great white chief in his African restaurant. This would then be a world without trust, without faith, without unselfishness, without love—a world where everybody obeyed God because it paid them to do so. Horrors![21]

Perhaps, therefore, some who run away from discipleship do not do it out of badness but because of the impending demands of goodness. If so, this would be but another reason why all, at a later point, will openly—if sadly—acknowledge the perfect justice and mercy of God. (Mosiah 16:1; Alma 12:15.)

The meek leader will act boldly and courageously when such is called for. It was needed when Brigham Young confronted Sidney Rigdon in the latter's bid for power after Joseph's martyrdom. Of that moment, President Young said: "I sat down directly opposite him, and took hold of his hand. I looked him right in the face and asked him [a series of questions]....I felt delicate in asking elder Rigdon these questions, but I knew it was my duty to find out the secret of the whole matter. To evade answering the questions I put to him, he finally said dont crowd my feelings too much."[22] Yet Brigham did so out of duty—not malice. He explained: "I am willing that you should know that my feelings for Sidney Rigdon as a man, as a private citizen, are of the best kind. I have loved that man and always had the very best feelings for him; I have stood in defence of his life and his house in Kirtland, and have lain on the floor, night after night, and week after week, to defend him. There are those who are following Sidney for whom my heart is grieved, I esteem them as good citizens. But when it touches the salvation of the people, I am the man that walks to the line."[23] One of the brethren who was there at the special interview said that Sidney Rigdon "was determined not to let brother Young pull things out of him."[24]

Elder John Taylor observed how, with regard to Sidney Rigdon, the Twelve had "invited him frequently to their council and have shown every mark of esteem, deference and respect, which his long standing in the church, his years, his talent and his calling would entitle him to.—They [the Twelve] have been extremely solicitous to cultivate a friendly feeling,...but they [the Twelve] have a duty to God and to this church to perform; and whatever may be their personal predilections, prejudices or feelings; they feel bound by the relationship they sustain to this church and to God, to lay aside all private feelings and secondary considerations in the fulfillment of the great work they are called upon to perform."[25]

Apparently the experience in Missouri had an impact

upon Brother Rigdon in ways that did not cause him to be stronger or sweeter: rather, according to President Brigham Young, Elder Rigdon "said Jesus Christ was a fool to him in sufferings," referring to the time in Missouri.[26] Ironically, some of the earlier brethren felt that Elder Rigdon's speech on the preceding Fourth of July had done much to excite and provoke gross persecution.[27]

Nor does the meek leader forget the purpose of the Lord's work: to save, not count, souls. Did he who proposed to proceed so that "one soul shall not be lost" hope to impress? (Moses 4:1.) Had he been so long with the Father and yet not understood either the Father's purposes or style?

In the management of power, as in few other things, we will surely learn of Jesus. We will surely come to marvel at His meekness in the midst of His astonishing accomplishments. His place on the Father's right hand is fully deserved, a place to be approached by us only upon our knees. But long before our knees willingly bend, there must be genuine intellectual humility.

NOTES

1. Quoted in Barbara Tuchman, *The March of Folly*, p. 383.
2. Ibid., p. 381.
3. Ibid., p. 18.
4. Ibid.
5. Ibid., p. 383.
6. John Colville, *The Fringes of Power*, p. 79.
7. Robert Rhodes, ed., *Churchill Speaks*, p. 10.
8. Ted Morgan, *Churchill, Young Man in a Hurry, 1874-1915*, p. 175.
9. Ibid.
10. Rhodes, *Churchill Speaks*, p. 734.
11. The words "it mattereth not" or their equivalent can be a clue to great character. Similar words appear in other settings, coming from meek individuals: "I finish my message; and then *it matters not* whither I go, if it so be that I am saved." (Mosiah 13:9. Italics added.) "Now the last words which are written by Ether are these: Whether the Lord will that I be translated, or that I suffer the will of the Lord in the flesh, *it mattereth not*, if it so be that I am saved in the kingdom of God. Amen." (Ether 15:34. Italics added.) "If it be so, our God whom we serve is able to deliver us from the burning fiery furnace, and he will deliver us out of thine hand, O king. But *if not*, be it known unto thee, O king, that we will not serve thy gods, nor worship the golden image which thou hast set up." (Daniel 3:17–18. Italics added.)

12. Sara Bradford, *Disraeli,* p. 440.
13. Ibid., pp. 439, 521.
14. Bart McDowell, *Revolutionary War,* pp. 190–91.
15. Elizabeth Longford, *Wellington, Pillar of State,* p. 507.
16. Ibid.
17. Ibid., p. 31.
18. Elizabeth Longford, *Wellington, the Years of the Sword,* p. 586.
19. Longford, *Wellington, Pillar of State,* p. 31.
20. "We Thank Thee, O God, for a Prophet," *Hymns,* 1985, no. 19.
21. Alan Hayward, *God Is,* p. 134.
22. *Times and Seasons* 5 (September 15, 1844): 648.
23. Ibid.
24. Ibid., p. 661.
25. Ibid.
26. *Times and Seasons* 5 (October 1, 1844): 666.
27. Ibid., p. 667.

Chapter Three

HUMBLENESS
OF MIND

"Put on therefore, as the elect of God, holy and beloved, ... humbleness of mind, meekness, long-suffering." (Colossians 3:12)

M eekness of mind is essential, salvationally. It is likewise vital if we are to experience true intellectual growth and to heighten our understanding of the great realities of the universe. Such meekness is a friend to, not a foe of, true education. It is noteworthy that Luke made these comments about Moses: "And Moses was learned in all the wisdom of the Egyptians, and was mighty in words and in deeds." (Acts 7:22.) Moses was a learned man, but, very significantly, he was also "very meek, above all the men which were upon the face of the earth." (Numbers 12:3.)

Moses' ministry, of course, can be viewed merely as an exercise in political science or solely in terms of his leadership style. But so much that matters will then be missed if we do not savor all the data, including that which has been restored concerning Moses, such as the significance of his intellectual inquiries of the Lord atop a high mountain before the Exodus.[1] (Moses 1.) If we miss the significance of such episodes, Moses' being atop the Mount of Transfiguration much later in a spiritually elite gathering will not be fully appreciated.

If we look only at the outside things, we will miss what the scriptures tell us of the process of deepening discipleship. It was similar with regard to Joseph Smith. One can spend time musing over the events concerning the *Nauvoo Expositor* and overlook the significance of what happened in the upper room of the Nauvoo general store, where Joseph chose to forgo public and ceremonial duties in order to finish his work on the Book of Abraham. There, too, the Prophet prepared, instructed, and blessed the Twelve for hours. Anyone thus preoccupied with such strategic substance and with such transcending things as Joseph was should not be judged solely by tactical errors, though these can be noted in an instructive—not an obsessive—way.

The meek understand all this and have delight, not difficulty, in understanding this request from a prophet: "Condemn me not because of mine imperfection, neither my father, because of his imperfection, neither them who have written before him; but rather give thanks unto God that he hath made manifest unto you our imperfections, that ye may learn to be more wise than we have been." (Mormon 9:31.)

The meek make way for divine data even when these can be both dislocating of pride and startling to the intellect. The interactiveness of the Lord with His prophets, crisscrossing and arcing through the ages as these relationships do, is not surprising. The involvements, for instance, of Jehovah-Jesus with Moses included not only the earlier tutoring in Sinai before, during, and after the Exodus, but also in the much later supernal events atop the Mount of Transfiguration. Paul grasped that it was Jesus whom Moses chose—the reproach of Christ rather than the riches and honors of the courts of Pharaoh. (Hebrews 11:24–26.)

When Philip went to Nathanael, he was bursting with excitement about the Messiah. Meek Philip said he had found the One about whom Moses and the prophets had spoken. (John 1:45.) But the unmeek majority could not, or would not, see the connection. Yet Jesus spoke openly of it, providing His answer to the "great question": "For had ye believed Moses, ye would have believed me: for he wrote of me. But if ye believe not his writings, how shall ye believe my words?" (John 5:45-47.)

The meek see the interactiveness of all scriptures: "For behold, this is written for the intent that ye may believe that; and if ye believe that ye will believe this also; and if ye believe this ye will know concerning your fathers, and also the marvelous works which were wrought by the power of God among them." (Mormon 7:9.)

Happily, in our time many added and precious words of Moses have been restored to us through the Prophet Joseph Smith. The meek will search—not just read or quote from—all scriptures. (John 5:39.) They discover "new" verses of scripture in their very next reading, being now ready for that which has been there, unnoticed, all along.

Once Paul understood about Jesus' being the Messiah and overcame his narrow and pharisaical view of things, he became an earnest and most effective witness for the Savior; then he had to contend with the same narrowness in his audiences. No wonder Paul preached with such great vigor about how Moses had spoken of the coming of the Messiah and the Christ—"That Christ should suffer, and that he should be the first that should rise from the dead, and should shew light unto the people, and to the Gentiles." (Acts 26:23.)

Paul saw, again and again, how to most Jews Jesus of Nazareth was a "stumbling block." Later in his ministry, he saw a dual form of rejection: to most Greeks, Jesus was "foolishness." (1 Corinthians 1:23.) Only the meek—then and now—have ears to hear and eyes to see and the courage to receive "repentance to the acknowledging of the truth." (2 Timothy 2:25.)

The traditional advantages of genuine learning are brought forth in promises and urgings and instructions from the Lord: "Whatever principle of intelligence we attain unto in this life, it will rise with us in the resurrection." (D&C 130:18.) "It is impossible for a man to be saved in ignorance." (D&C 131:6.) "And as all have not faith, seek ye diligently and teach one another words of wisdom; yea, seek ye out of the best books words of wisdom; seek learning, even by study and also by faith." (D&C 88:118.)

These and other scriptures make abundantly clear the Lord's commitment to genuine education, but an education that is balanced by including more and more about the great spiritual realities of the universe. These realities bear upon the "great question" and the answer to it: the centrality of Jesus Christ to our understanding of ourselves, of life, of Heavenly Father's plan of salvation, and of the purpose and design of this planet—indeed, the universe. Otherwise, as well-educated Paul warned, the indiscriminate approach to learning finds persons mistaking comparative piles of chaff for kernels of wheat, and, therefore, such are "ever learning, and never able to come to the knowledge of the truth." (2 Timothy 3:7.)

Thus great stress must be placed upon the need for intellectual meekness—"humbleness of mind." Meekness is not a passive attribute that merely deflects discourtesy. Instead, it involves intellectual activism. "For Ezra had prepared his heart to seek the law of the Lord, and to do it, and to teach in Israel statutes and judgments." (Ezra 7:10. See also 2 Chronicles 19:3; 20:33.)

Meek Nephi decried the passivity of those who "will not search knowledge, nor understand great knowledge, when it is given unto them in plainness." (2 Nephi 32:7.) Alas, most are quite content with a superficial understanding or a general awareness of spiritual things. (Alma 10:5-6.) This condition may reflect either laziness or the busyness incident to the pressing cares of the world.

But there is another explanation for the reticence to search and to understand. Some individuals are perceptive enough to understand that with great knowledge come great responsibilities. Great knowledge in response to the great questions will alter how we view both great and small things, if we are intellectually honest. Therefore, while aversion to searching great knowledge exists because of conceptual inadequacy and also because people are lazy and busy, it likewise exists and persists because some do not want the great responsibilities that come with great knowledge. For some, at least, rejecting or ignoring transcending truths is an act of deliberate avoidance, even running away.

Doctrinal disclosures do make demands of us. Such disclosures, therefore, are not something to be noted and then filed away. Meekness, with its capacity for gratefulness, causes individuals to search, explore, and ponder great knowledge. They are they who, on occasion, are taken to mountaintops. However, this usually occurs not as a result of passivity on the valley floor, but only after their own arduous climbing. Then such persons are helped, "after all they can do." (2 Nephi 25:23.)

From the very beginning, Jesus, the Meek Volunteer—who long, long ago said, "Here am I, send me" (Abraham 3:23)—set the example for us with regard to meekness. He knew beforehand, *intellectually,* that His acceptance of the atoning role entailed awesome responsibilities, responsibilities that would eventually lead to His knowing *experientially* in Gethsemane and on Calvary as the weight of the yoke of our sins, sicknesses, pains, and infirmities fell upon him. (2 Nephi 9:21; Alma 7:11-12.) On Calvary, Christ's previous *knowing* required *doing*—until it was "finished." (John 19:30.) Significantly, it was not "finished" until He had felt "forsaken," as evidenced by the great soul cry from the cross. (Mark 15:34.)

For centuries, Jesus had known that when He was burning with thirst, He would receive vinegar, and also that He would come to feel forsaken, just as the Psalmist prophesied: "My God, my God, why hast thou forsaken me? why art thou so far from helping me?" (Psalm 22:1.) "They gave me also gall for my meat; and in my thirst they gave me vinegar to drink." (Psalm 69:21.)

Yet Jesus overcame in the crucible that was Gethsemane and Calvary. He was meekly and spiritually submissive because He had first been intellectually submissive. Having first made room for great knowledge and great understanding, He later made room for greater responsibilities and awesome burdens.

Unlike Him, some of us run from the implications and responsibilities of the doctrines in which we believe. Even when "the judgments of God stare [us] in the face" (Helaman 4:23), some of us "spurn at the doings of the Lord" (3 Nephi 29:4).

Thus meekness is so vital—not only to introduce us to new knowledge but also to put down pride, which could keep us from facing and submitting to the implications of that knowledge, especially when responsibilities previously agreed to and understood must be finally met and endured well to the end.

Our capacity for gladness of mind also turns on how highly developed our humbleness of mind is. The events, for instance, atop the Mount of Transfiguration were not for intellectual and spiritual "undergraduates." And Calvary admitted but an exclusive class of One!

Gospel gladness can be experienced for many reasons. It was present in the joyous shouting during the premortal presentation of the plan of salvation. (Job 38:7.) It was there at the deliverance of Israel at the Red Sea when Moses and the children of Israel also sang a special song unto the Lord. (Exodus 15:1-2.) Gospel gladness can be present when receiving emancipating truths as when the Psalmist exclaimed, "Such knowledge is too wonderful for me" (Psalm 139:6); or, as with Ammon, in rejoicing over being part of the Lord's work when one's "heart is brim with joy" (Alma 26:11); or in those precious times of enjoying the truths of the faith, while momentarily resting from defending the faith. Whenever, this gladness is always facilitated by meekness, and it brings refreshment, so that we will not be wearied and faint in our minds. (Hebrews 12:3.)

Doctrinal disclosures can evoke gospel gladness; King Benjamin was correct when he said that "great knowledge" brings "great joy." (Mosiah 5:4.)

There are small truths as well to help us.

There are, for instance, a number of words in the scriptures that we assume we know the meaning of, but in our casualness we fail to search them. One such word occurs in the revelation given to the Prophet Joseph Smith in Liberty Jail. It declares that true leadership requires "reproving *betimes* with sharpness, when moved upon by the Holy Ghost; and then showing forth afterwards an increase of love toward him whom thou hast reproved, lest he esteem thee to be his enemy." (D&C 121:43. Italics added.) Most of us casually assume the word *betimes* means "from time to time," or occasionally. *Betimes* actually means "early on."

If we both identify a need early and are moved upon by the Holy Ghost to act before pride has hardened our attitudes, we have a greater likelihood of success. Our effectiveness in working with others depends not only upon our meekness but also upon theirs, and mutual meekness is more apt to be present "early on" rather than later.

Contrariwise, without intellectual and spiritual nourishment, instead of gladness there is weariness and murmuring. Why do we murmur? In part, as with provincial Laman and Lemuel, "because they knew not the dealings of that God who had created them." (1 Nephi 2:12.) Nephi, on the other hand, received an extra errand from the Lord and was "favored of the Lord" because he had not murmured. (1 Nephi 3:6.)

Lack of meekness begets lack of knowledge, which, in turn, begets murmuring, and so the cycle goes on and on. For a few brief moments, Laman and Lemuel were apparently humble, and they even asked questions. (1 Nephi 15:20; 16:5.) This all happened after some splendid but straightforward teaching by Nephi about God's plans for the Jews and the plan of salvation. Otherwise, Laman and Lemuel's episodic meekness and humility seem to have required rescuing events, followed by a loss of humility as soon as memory of the rescue faded from consciousness or as soon as new demands pressed to the fore, submerging what they knew of "the dealings of that God who had created them." (1 Nephi 2:12.)

Feasting upon the word of Christ can provide needed adrenalin for deepening and maintaining discipleship. Joseph Smith called one especially nourishing disclosure (Moses 1) a "precious morsel." These disclosures involve more than intellectual calisthenics; they push out the borders of our understanding and can restructure our understanding of ourselves, the world, and the universe, teaching us things we "never had supposed." (Moses 1:10.)[2]

If we will feast upon the gospel's transcending truths and apply them, we will not be "wearied and faint in [our] minds." (Hebrews 12:3.) Fainting intellectually will not occur when we are properly nourished. We can have assurances to sustain us that will keep us from fainting in our minds. The Prophet Joseph Smith taught: "Such was, and always will be, the situation of the saints of God, that unless they have an actual knowledge that the course they are pursuing is according to the will of God they will grow weary in their minds, and faint."[3]

With such intellectual and spiritual nourishment, we can not only rejoice, but, significantly, we will also "be filled with love towards God and all men." (Mosiah 2:4.) People fatigue is dissipated by love and learning: "And it came to pass that peace and the love of God was restored again among the people; and they searched the scriptures." (Jacob 7:23.) Marvelous outcomes flow from inspired insights from the Spirit or scripture. Refreshment, renewal, and reassurance follow. There is also a keener sense, on our part, that we are in fact surrounded "with so great a cloud of witnesses." (Hebrews 12:1.) We become a part of a vast community of believers that transcends time and space, providing precious perspective.

Our feelings on such occasions can be full, as we rejoice over the validity, the simplicity, and the beauty of God's loving and enclosing gospel plan. The knowledge we have may yet be comparatively meager but correct. Concerning such transcending truths, we may say they are "too wonderful for me." (Job 42:3.) But such truths are received only by those possessed of humbleness of mind, though they restructure or restore our understanding of "things as they really are." (Jacob 4:13.) Indeed, we can "have faith in Christ because of [our] meekness" (Moroni 7:39), and, "in the spirit of meekness," confess Him "before the world" (D&C 124:18).

How blessed we are, for instance, to understand that "man was also in the beginning with God." (D&C 93:29.) We are the spirit children of God, who created us, yet we had in some essential respect—said Joseph Smith in the King Follett sermon—"no beginning" and are "eternal." (See also D&C 93:29; Abraham 3:18.) As carriers of immortal genes, we are not left to believe in an *ex nihilo* creation with its painful dilemmas and dichotomies.

We are blessed too with moral agency, without which there would be no growth and no capacity to have true joy. Though we each may sin, we are not haunted with an overhanging sense of "original sin" about which we can do nothing. (Moses 6:54; Moroni 8:15-16.) By revelation, we know that the Lord told Adam: "Behold I have

forgiven thee thy transgression in the Garden of Eden."
(Moses 6:53.) Thus, we are accountable for our "own sins,
and not for Adam's transgression." (Article of Faith 2.) In
fact, "because that Adam fell, we are." (Moses 6:48.)
Furthermore, "men are, that they might have joy." (2
Nephi 2:25.)

We do not live in an unexplainable world either. We
need neither be drenched in despair nor resignedly "eat,
drink, and be merry, for tomorrow we die." (2 Nephi
28:7-8.) Instead, we are volunteer participants in God's
plan of salvation (Moses 6:62), which plan required the
rescue mission by the Great Volunteer, Jesus Christ.
Through Him and His atonement, there is an assured
resurrection awaiting—not extinction. A worldwide
millennium is impending, preceded by much misery and
destruction, not total world annihilation. Divine determination so insures, and "there is nothing that the Lord
shall take in his heart to do but what he will do it."
(Abraham 3:17.)

We are blessed to know, perhaps uniquely among
today's groups, that in the distant dawn of human
history, "the Gospel began to be preached, from the
beginning, being declared by holy angels sent forth from
the presence of God, and by his own voice, and by the gift
of the Holy Ghost. And thus all things were confirmed
unto Adam, by an holy ordinance, and the Gospel
preached, and a decree sent forth, that it should be in the
world, until the end thereof; and thus it was." (Moses
5:58-59.)

In this proving experience, those with meek eyes can
see the evidences of divine design. These evidences are
neither incidental nor occasional, but "all things are
created and made to bear record" of God. (Moses 6:63.)
The Holy Ghost testifies to us individually of the truth of
these things. But without this oil in the lamp, which
cannot finally be borrowed, we will not know and will

not have the requisite humbleness of mind. We so much need meekness because in the midst of all these things, "the Lord seeth fit to chasten his people; yea, he trieth their patience and their faith." (Mosiah 23:21.)

Faith, works, and ordinances are all essential: none of these is adequate alone. Life is so designed that "all these things shall give [us] experience" and can be for our good. (D&C 122:7.) Compared to the available eternal blessings, however, mortal stresses, grim as these may be, shall be "but for a small moment." (D&C 122:4.) We are surely to be stretched, but we will also be steadied, for the Lord's grace "is sufficient for the meek." (Ether 12:26.) Families, doctrines, scriptures, and temples will also be part of such steadying.

We are so blessed to know there is a tutoring and loving Father-God, not some impersonal life-force, nor a distracted, absentee monarch presiding somewhere in space. Indeed, the Lord tutoreth in tenderness, and blessed are the tutored.

Such tenderness is even reflected in the voice of the Lord, which is neither harsh nor loud—but piercing to the center of the soul. (3 Nephi 11:3.) Helaman's sons, Nephi and Lehi, heard a "voice of perfect mildness, as if it had been a whisper, and it did pierce even unto the very soul." (Helaman 5:30.)

The Lord is a willing guest when invited by our spiritual readiness. Three years before Adam's death, when he gathered his righteous posterity in the valley of Adam-ondi-Ahman to bestow a father's last blessing, there was a Special Guest in attendance:

> And the Lord appeared unto them, and they rose up and blessed Adam, and called him Michael, the prince, the archangel.
>
> And the Lord administered comfort unto Adam, and said unto him: I have set thee to be at the head; a multitude of nations shall come of thee, and thou art a prince over them forever.

And Adam stood up in the midst of the congregation; and, notwithstanding he was bowed down with age, being full of the Holy Ghost, predicted whatsoever should befall his posterity unto the latest generation. (D&C 107:54–56.)

Someday that same special valley will echo again with the sounds of joyous, representative reunion! (D&C 116; Daniel 7:13.)

The greater our gospel gladness, the more the Father and His Son rejoice:

In that hour Jesus rejoiced in spirit, and said, I thank thee, O Father, Lord of heaven and earth, that thou hast hid these things from the wise and prudent, and hast revealed them unto babes: even so, Father; for so it seemed good in thy sight. (Luke 10:21.)

And now, behold, my joy is great, even unto fulness, because of you, and also this generation; yea, and even the Father rejoiceth, and also all the holy angels, because of you and this generation; for none of them are lost. (3 Nephi 27:30.)

And it came to pass that when Jesus had made an end of praying unto the Father, he arose; but so great was the joy of the multitude that they were overcome. And it came to pass that Jesus spake unto them, and bade them arise. And they arose from the earth, and he said unto them: Blessed are ye because of your faith. And now behold, my joy is full.

And when he had said these words, he wept, and the multitude bare record of it, and he took their little children, one by one, and blessed them, and prayed unto the Father for them. And when he had done this he wept again. (3 Nephi 17:18–22.)

The Father and Son desire to share even further their joy with us. "For this cause ye shall have fulness of joy; and ye shall sit down in the kingdom of my Father; yea, your joy shall be full, even as the Father hath given me fulness of joy; and ye shall be even as I am." (3 Nephi 28:10.) Our share in such joy is wholly different from the fleeting satisfactions of the world that come from satisfaction for a season in "the works of men." Even when sincere and significant, those satisfactions only last "for a season," for He who has known full and true joy has so said. (3 Nephi 27:11.)

How blessed we are, therefore, to experience such gospel gladness, as when, meekly, we come to know what Paul called "the deep things of God" (1 Corinthians 2:10), or learn of what Jacob called "things as they really are, ... things as they really will be; ... things ... manifested unto us plainly, for the salvation of our souls" (Jacob 4:13). These transcending truths do bring us a stunning perspective, a "knowledge of things as they are, and as they were, and as they are to come." (D&C 93:24.) These transcending truths restructure our understanding of ourselves and of the universe and bring within our view resplendent reality.

To be seen only by those who have eyes to see, these flakes of fire are embedded in the holy scriptures. There these transcending truths may appear in the midst of the routine lineage history. (Compare Ether 6:14 and 12:27.) They may be found within chronologies, genealogies, and duties (D&C 107:53-57), or may follow upon now dated economic data (Mosiah 23:20-21). When encountered, their sudden richness is so breathtaking and light-intensive that, like radioactive materials, they must be handled with great care. They both light up the mind and infuse joy into the soul. (Alma 19:6.)

All true scripture is of God and for a purpose, but encountering certain verses is like walking in the woods and coming suddenly upon what C. S. Lewis called a patch of "god light"—an illuminated place in the woods of our experiences. Then there is a special surge of gospel gladness. The weariness of mind quickly departs.

Such sudden light can even restructure our understanding of reality and put our past, puny efforts in perspective. One wonders, for instance, if whatever occurred to Thomas Aquinas in December 1273 was an example of what Moses called things he "never had supposed." (Moses 1:10.) After the experience, Aquinas's prolific writing ceased. He wrote: "I can do no more; such things have been revealed to me that all I have written seems as straw, and I now await the end of my life."[4] Three months later he died.

Intellectual meekness is a particular challenge. Without it, we are not intellectually open to things we "never had supposed." Alas, some have reached provincial conclusions and do not really want to restructure their understanding of things. Some wish to be neither shaken nor expanded by new spiritual data. It is quite a step, for instance, to move from passive belief in an immaterial, impersonal life-force god to a belief in a God who is indeed our Heavenly Father and in whose image we have been created. This latter God, the only true and living God, behaves just like a Perfect Father, loving us, reproving us, stretching us, teaching us, and, yes, making demands of us!

It is quite a step as well from concluding in favor of the randomness and inexplicableness of human existence to believing in an ordered plan and in divine design. Obviously, such sweeping perspectives as the latter have an impact on daily life, on how we see others, and on how we should spend our time, talent, and treasure.

It is no small journey to go from despising believers to becoming one of them. This was Paul's challenge with regard to the Christians. He moved from disapproval and condescension of them to community with them. It is also a major move from using one's doubts as a cover for errant behavior to having those doubts taken away by truth with the resultant need to humbly alter one's behavior.

In all of these ways, the moments of truth keep on arriving. Selfishness, for instance, is made to stare, eye to eye, at the substantive requirements of the second commandment. Without sufficient meekness, however, selfishness will at first blink, close its eyes, and then turn away. Critics who have held so many cloaks, when they have not been doing the stoning themselves, and who have come to find their position "pleasing unto the carnal mind," will not be able to desist and put down the cloaks, as Paul did, unless they have meekness.

Meekness emancipates us from the prison of the secular mind, the proud mind. As C. S. Lewis wrote, "Their prison is only in their minds, yet they are in that prison; and so afraid of being taken in that they can not be taken out."[5]

There are so many prodigals who lack the meekness and the intellectual clarity to do what the prodigal son did. Saying, in effect, "Living like this is ridiculous!," the prodigal son "came to himself." He realized how much better off he would be to return to his father. He did not ponder, "What will they say? Will anyone come out to meet me?" Instead, he arose and went home. Being sufficiently meek to feel caused him to think, and humbleness of mind saved his soul. (Luke 15:11–32.)

Those who are proud of mind demand extrinsic evidence. The Lord told the Prophet Joseph Smith, "Behold, if they will not believe my words, they would not believe you, my servant Joseph, if it were possible that you should show them all these things which I have committed unto you." (D&C 5:7.) On the other hand, those who are humble and meek seek, by faith, to understand truth. They are comfortable with intrinsic as well as extrinsic evidence. They know that "faith is the substance of things hoped for, the evidence of things not seen." (Hebrews 11:1.)

NOTES

1. On one such supernal occasion, taught the Prophet Joseph Smith, Moses received his endowments. (Andrew F. Ehat and Lyndon W. Cook, *The Words of Joseph Smith*, p. 120.)

2. There is another intriguing dimension of meekness that has to do with the opening of the mind to sweeping impressions, even those not essentially spiritual. Wellington, on one occasion, spoke of his generalship in these words: "There is a curious thing that one feels sometimes; when you are considering a subject, suddenly a whole train of reasoning comes before you like a flash of light; you see it all (moving his hand as if something appeared before him, his eye with its brightest expression), yet it takes you perhaps two years to put on paper all that has occurred to your mind in an instant. Every part of the subject, the bearing of all the parts upon each other, and all the consequences are there before you." (Elizabeth Longford, *Wellington, Pillar of State,* p. 506.) Scientists sometimes experience such sudden infusions of insight.

3. *Lectures on Faith,* lecture 6, no. 4.

4. *Great Books: Aquinas I & II,* p. vi.

5. C. S. Lewis, *The Last Battle,* p. 140.

Chapter Four

THE DEADLY SIN
OF PRIDE

"Therefore pride compasseth them about as a chain."
(Psalm 73:6)

Just as meekness is in all our virtues, so pride is in all our sins. Whatever its momentary and alluring guise, pride is the enemy, "the first of the sins."[1]

According to *The Interpreter's Dictionary of the Bible*, "at least six Hebrew roots contain the idea of pride, and almost all of them mean 'to lift up,' 'to be high.'" These are translated into English as *arrogance, loftiness, presumption, boasting*. A number of Old Testament passages "point toward pride as the virtual ground of sin."[2]

Not only must Latter-day Saints be concerned about pride in all its usual manifestations, but we need also to be particularly on guard against that pride which arises out of our sought-for spiritual status or our achievements, such as they are, having come thus far. Thus it is always important for us to remember Paul's counsel: "Wherefore let him that thinketh he standeth take heed lest he fall." (1 Corinthians 10:12.)

Pride should be a real concern for those already converted since, unless one is meek, "by and by he is offended" because of the word. (Matthew 13:21.) The concern over what has been called spiritual pride was a concern of Jesus, who addressed a parable "unto certain which trusted in themselves that they were righteous, and despised others." (Luke 18:9.)

The pervasiveness of pride and the degree to which it is persistent in our lives must ever put us on guard, reminding us, as did Paul, not to be "highminded," for we "stand by faith." (Romans 11:20.) Faith dissolves very quickly when meekness disappears and pride takes over. Thus, if pride is "the first of the sins," then meekness is a premiere virtue.

Henry Fairlie, in writing of the pervasiveness of pride, observed that it is "an assertion of self-sufficiency—a denial of one's need for community with others, which is in fact a form of selfishness, since it is always accompanied by a refusal of one's obligation of community with others."[3] Fairlie also observed that pride "is a sin of neglect: It causes us to ignore others. It is a sin of aggression: It provokes us to hurt others. It is a sin of condescension: It makes us patronize others."[4] This correlates with a prophetic condemnation of a proud, insensitive, and unnoticing people: "Why do ye adorn yourselves with that which hath no life, and yet suffer the hungry, and the needy, and the naked, and the sick and the afflicted to pass by you, and notice them not?" (Mormon 8:39.)

The gospel seeks to make us a community of saints, a city on a hill, but pride and selfishness produce just the opposite result. As Fairlie pointed out, "If all the sins are causes of solitariness, Pride is the first begetter of it.... There is today evidence of this all around us, in the vacancy of lives that are lived only for themselves."[5]

One reason to be particularly on guard against pride is that "the devilish strategy of Pride is that it attacks us, not in our weakest points, but in our strongest. It is pre-eminently the sin of the noble mind."[6] Not only of the noble mind, but also of the semirighteous.

Those of us who are too comfortable with our market-place economy, with all of its efficiencies and advantages, need to beware of what can happen when the marketplace mentality colludes and conspires to produce an even more proud, sensual, and selfish people. In such circumstances, Fairlie warned, "when people begin to look for exotic and terrible forms of self-pleasing, our commercial societies are at once in the marketplace to supply them."[7]

Pride is decried in its early stages by the Lord and His prophets. Given the gravity of pride, prophets are quick to notice even its first protrusions, because such warning signs foretell of dissensions that can grow quickly and steadily like a fungus. We read of such problems among the Nephites: "Now it came to pass in the forty and third year of the reign of the judges, there was no contention among the people of Nephi save it were a little pride which was in the church, which did cause some little dissensions among the people, which affairs were settled in the ending of the forty and third year.... And it came to pass that the fifty and second year ended in peace also, save it were the exceedingly great pride which had gotten into the hearts of the people; and it was because of their exceedingly great riches and their prosperity in the land; and it did grow upon them from day to day." (Helaman 3:1, 36.)

In view of later events, one wonders about the warning given to Oliver Cowdery about his need to "beware of pride." (D&C 23:1.) Oliver had contributed so very much, yet his later loss of place in the kingdom, according to Brigham Young, occurred because he was proud. "I have seen men who belonged to this kingdom," President Young said, "and who really thought that if they were not associated with it, it could not progress. One man especially, whom I now think of, who was peculiarly gifted in self-reliance and general ability. He said as much to the Prophet Joseph a number of times as to say that if he left this kingdom, it could not progress any further. I speak of Oliver Cowdery. He forsook it, and it still rolled on, and still triumphed over every opposing foe, and bore all safely all those who clung to it."[8] Yet, happily, Oliver was meek enough both to humbly rejoin the Church and to testify, just before his death, of its truthfulness.

Scriptural warnings often couple pride and selfishness. (See, for example, D&C 56:8.) Pride can be characteristic of a whole race and will cause one of the hingepoint happenings in human history. As far as the spread of the gospel is concerned, the time will come when the Lord will take His gospel elsewhere from the proud and resistant Gentiles. He told the Nephites: "At that day when the Gentiles shall sin against my gospel, and shall reject the fulness of my gospel, and shall be lifted up in the pride of their hearts above all nations, and above all the people of the whole earth, and shall be filled with all manner of lyings, and of deceits, and of mischiefs, and all manner of hypocrisy, and murders, and priestcrafts, and whoredoms, and of secret abominations; and if they shall do all those things, and shall reject the fulness of my gospel, behold, saith the Father, I will bring the fulness of my gospel from among them." (3 Nephi 16:10.)

Before the millennial time when the arrogancy of the proud will cease, the Gentiles will be in a circumstance of "great pride, unto boasting, and unto great swelling, envyings, strifes, malice, persecutions, and murders, and all manner of iniquities." (Helaman 13:22.)

The gigantic, global collapse that is yet to come will not be that of a failing stockmarket, but the fall of hardened mindsets and collective pride when it all finally tumbles. Nephi testified: "It came to pass that I saw and bear record, that the great and spacious building was the pride of the world; and it fell, and the fall thereof was exceedingly great. And the angel of the Lord spake unto me again, saying: Thus shall be the destruction of all nations, kindreds, tongues, and people, that shall fight against the twelve apostles of the Lamb." (1 Nephi 11:36.)

However "large and spacious" that building may be, it is a third-rate hotel whose occupants are all dressed up but have no place to go. (1 Nephi 8:27.) Thus, one day He who was raised on the third day will raze this third-rate hotel! Furthermore, the time will come when "the Son of man shall send forth his angels, and they shall gather out of his kingdom all things that offend, and them which do iniquity." (Matthew 13:41.) Thus, rather than being offended, we should take care not to offend.

Happily, there are some on-the-record and heartening moments when a whole people have been checked as to their pride. For example, "after Alma...established the church at Sidom,...the people were checked as to the pride of their hearts, and began to humble themselves before God, and began to assemble themelves together at their sanctuaries to worship God before the altar, watching and praying continually, that they might be delivered from Satan, and from death, and from destruction." (Alma 15:17.)

Dissenters and defectors even have a special form of pride, losing so quickly their appreciation for what they already have. In Alma we read: "And thus we can plainly discern, that after a people have been once enlightened by the Spirit of God, and have had great knowledge of things pertaining to righteousness, and then have fallen away into sin and transgression, they become more hardened, and thus their state becomes worse than though they had never known these things." (Alma 24:30.)

The Prophet Joseph Smith taught: "Strange as it may appear at first thought, yet it is no less strange than true, that notwithstanding all the professed determination to live godly, apostates after turning from the faith of Christ, unless they have speedily repented, have sooner or later fallen into the snares of the wicked one, and have been left destitute of the Spirit of God, to manifest their wickedness in the eyes of multitudes. From apostates the faithful have received the severest persecutions."[9]

Pride can begin incipiently and gradually, but with

THE DEADLY SIN OF PRIDE

frightening prospects, as Joseph Smith pointed out: "The moment we revolt at anything which comes from God, the devil takes power."[10]

The case of James Covill illustrates the importance of meekness with regard to submissiveness. (See D&C 39–40.) Covill offered himself to the Lord, promising to do whatever he was asked to do. Though he was called to work in Ohio, he apparently had other ideas; it was just a short time until he had broken his promise to the Lord. Covill's anticipatory fear of persecution—before any persecution even commenced—may have dissolved such meekness as he had. Besides, the meek can see persecution with wider eyes. Brigham Young recalled: "I told the people that if they [those who opposed the Church] would let us alone, and not raise any persecutions, we would go peaceably along among the people and preach to them; but that just as sure as they fought us and opposed this work we would actually revolutionize the world a great deal quicker than if they let us alone. I have stuck to that faith ever since; for every time that there has been an opposition raised against this work, God has caused it to swell like seed in the ground."[11]

Jonah sought to avoid going to Nineveh where he was called, seeking instead to go to Tarshish. Yet it was in Nineveh that he received one of the great lessons of his life that provided such an insight for us all. The meek will go where they are called; their obedience will see them through when reason and past experiences, by themselves, are not enough to sustain them. There are on record more examples of *individuals* who have meekly turned around in response to a call to serve or to repent or to follow divine instruction than examples of *groups* doing such. Nineveh, however, is a dramatic exception to the pattern, as are some brief turnarounds in the Book of Mormon. It is a heroic thing for individuals to reverse themselves, their attitudes, and their patterns of behavior in order to pursue discipleship; it is truly remarkable for a whole people to do so.

Self-control depends upon meekness. Otherwise, "an angry man stirreth up strife, and a furious man aboundeth in transgression." (Proverbs 29:22.) A furious man is out of control. Individuals who are meek may not always decipher what is happening to them or around them; however, even though they do not "know the meaning of all things," they know that the Lord loves them. (1 Nephi 11:17.) They may feel overwhelmed, but they are not out of control. In those moments, it is important for us to remember His counsel: "Be still, and know that I am God." (Psalm 46:10.) Articulate discipleship has a dimension of silent certitude!

The *rest* promised by Jesus, though not including an absence of adversity or tutoring, does give us that peace which flows from humbleness of mind. The meek management of power and responsibility relieves us of the heavy chains of pride and protects us from the fatigue of being offended—to note but a few benefits. There are many persons just waiting to be offended: certain they will not be treated fairly, they almost invite the verification of their expectation.

President Harold B. Lee, in describing a meek person, observed that such an individual "is not easily provoked or irritated, and is forbearing under injury or annoyance." The meek man, he added, is "the man of complete self-mastery."[12]

In the topsy-turvy last days, it is important to realize that as "the eternal purposes of the Lord shall roll on," His disciples will surely know what it is to be tumbled. (Mormon 8:22.) It will be no time to be proud, especially when the tumblings may not at the moment seem purposeful. Yet the Lord's work will roll on; His meek disciples will understand.

Rocks of offense or stones of stumbling keep the

proud from making spiritual progress. No less destructive is what might be called the gravel of grumpiness, which keeps us off balance and annoyingly turns ankles. Even though we do not fully fall or stumble, we progress more slowly, painfully, and fitfully. The meek, however, make stepping-stones of stumbling blocks.

In moments of truth, when meekness matters, other forces, including pride, flow into the chemistry of that moment. Take, for instance, the matter of receiving correct counsel, whether given by a spouse, a family member, a friend, or a Church leader. Often the counsel, even when spoken in love, is resisted by the recipient who—chained by pride—focuses instead upon the imperfections of the person giving the counsel.

In another situation, the recipient may have much pride in the position he or she has already taken and refuse to deny himself or herself the continuation of that conduct, lifestyle, or attitude, which denial is at the heart of the solution. However, those who fear losing face cannot have His image in their countenances. (Alma 5:14.)

In yet another circumstance, the recipient may, instead of listening to the counsel given, be nursing some past grievance upon which he or she would prefer to focus rather than the real issue at hand.

Whatever the case, experience suggests that recipients of counsel may at the moment of truth feel one or more of these and other restraining forces at work. One force would, by itself, be enough in the absence of meekness, but several combined make meekness crucial. No wonder pride is such a chain! It can be a spreading and encircling chain, "a root of bitterness springing up [to] trouble you, and thereby many be defiled." (Hebrews 12:15.)

In such settings, experience also suggests the importance not only of meekness but also of the presence of the Spirit. Neither advice-giver nor circumstances can be perfect. Only the Spirit can leap across such deficiencies and convey the message lovingly and yet forcefully. The Lord told the elders of the Church in 1831, "Why is it that ye cannot understand and know, that he that receiveth the word by the Spirit of truth receiveth it as it is preached by the Spirit of truth? Wherefore, he that preacheth and he that receiveth, understand one another, and both are edified and rejoice together." (D&C 50:21-22.)

Absent mutual meekness, the counsel given may not only go unheeded, but, in fact, may even be resented.

Not only are there individual moments of truth, but there are also collective. As we are meek, we will have a perspective about that moment yet to come when the "whole human family of Adam" will stand before the judgment seat of Christ. (Mormon 3:20.) But with meekness also comes sober realization that we are our "own judges, whether to do good or evil." (Alma 41:7.) If we are meek, our minds will not be darkened, and we can judge rightly because it is "given unto [us] to judge, that [we] may know good from evil; and the way to judge is as plain...as the daylight from the dark night." (Moroni 7:15.) At that remarkable, sobering, and exhilarating moment, yet future, there will be no proud grievances with the justice of God. "The time shall come when all shall see the salvation of the Lord; when every nation, kindred, tongue, and people shall see eye to eye and shall confess before God that his judgments are just." (Mosiah 16:1.) Meanwhile, so far as this life is concerned, as the Prophet Joseph Smith said, "A man is his own tormentor." Likewise, "all will suffer until they obey Christ himself."[13] Pride merely defers the pain, like a debt that must be paid—now or later.

Bruising as the tumble off the peak of pride is, it may be necessary. Even then, one must be careful not to let despair continue the descent into the swamp of self-pity. Meekness enables us, after a tumble, to pick ourselves up but without putting others down blamefully. Since meekness lets us retain the rightful impressions of how blessed we are (so far as fundamental and eternal things are concerned), we are not then as easily offended by the disappointments of the day.

Arrogance and disobedience are cellmates. Granted, some disobedience stems from our not paying attention. Some, too, stems from casualness when seriousness is warranted. However, there are two other dimensions of disobedience: one occurs because we feel we know better than God what is needed or permitted; the other is willful wrongdoing with awareness.

The proud, so far as their own lives are concerned, along with those whom they adversely affect, mock the plan of salvation. (Jacob 6:8.) Those who boast of their independence from God are like the goldfish in a bowl who regards himself as self-sufficient. (See Mosiah 2:20–25.) Many of us do not even humbly regard the many unusual conditions that make human life on this planet at all possible. As the British scientist Alan Hayward has observed:

> Clearly, distance from the sun is very critical. Just a bit nearer to the sun, and Planet Earth's seas would soon be boiling; just a little farther out, and the whole world would become a frozen wilderness.... But that would not help us much if our orbit happened to be the wrong shape. All planets and satellites have orbits that are elliptical (oval) to some extent, and if our orbit were highly elliptical we should be at different distances from the sun at different times of the year. Then we should alternately freeze like Mars and fry like Venus once a year. Fortunately for us, our planet's orbit is very nearly a circle....
>
> The 21 percent of oxygen is another critical figure. Animals would have difficulty breathing if the oxygen content fell very far below that value. But an oxygen level much higher than this would also be disastrous, since the extra oxygen would act as a fire-raising material. Forests and grasslands would flare up every time lightning struck during a dry spell, and life on earth would become extremely hazardous.[14]

Praise God from whom all blessings flow!

For those who are grossly proud, the price of cooperation is sometimes domination by their pride. This is
reflective of another who said he would serve, but only
under certain conditions. Some actually exit this life,
their proudest boast being their refusal to submit; no
mortal could lead them. A most absurd posture of all, but
they will assume another posture one day. Alma taught:
"We must come forth and stand before him [God] in his
glory, and in his power, and in his might, majesty, and
dominion, and acknowledge to our everlasting shame
that all his judgments are just; that he is just in all his
works, and that he is merciful unto the children of men,
and that he has all power to save every man that
believeth on his name and bringeth forth fruit meet for
repentance." (Alma 12:15.) The inability of the proud to
follow the Perfect Leader is nothing to boast of, for it
means, in the end, that one cannot go where He is and
where full happiness abounds.

One of the faces of pride is murmuring. Often
murmuring is proud but cowardly. It often reflects
resentful complaints, such as the complaint of the people
of the Lord anciently concerning their having left a better
life in Egypt. The complaints concerned the poor land
they were inheriting and the absence of adequate water
and food. Some did "murmur in their tents." (Deuteronomy 1:27.) Murmuring of a different form occurred when
Jesus began to preach about Himself as "the bread of life"
and when He associated with sinners and publicans. He
urged his listeners, "Murmur not among yourselves."
(John 6:43.)

So it is that meekness is needed not alone to open to
us new understandings but also to keep us free and
intellectually active. Meekness with its emerging spiritual
resilience also provides a soft landing for hard doctrines.
Since it is the purgative to squeeze out paralyzing pride,

it is not a remedy so popular that many seek it over the counter. Compelling circumstances are usually necessary: "Therefore, blessed are they who humble themselves without being compelled to be humble; ... blessed is he that believeth in the word of God ... without stubbornness of heart, yea, without being brought to know the word, or even compelled to know, before they will believe." (Alma 32:16.)

Since murmuring has been such a challenge throughout human history, it is significant that meekness is also a cure for murmuring. Murmuring often consists of reluctant and resentful compliance, but only after we have grumbled a bit, only after we have made some points we think the Lord needs to hear, as if He needed to hear them. We are registering our pique but still "wearing the colors and staying on the team."

Meekness, however, feels no obligation to engage in murmuring. The ironies, the disappointments, and the injustices are felt by the meek, but the meek individual feels no need to lecture the Lord. After all, that individual has taken the Lord's yoke upon him to learn of Him, not the other way around!

Jesus taught parabolically how often people feel unjustly dealt with, even though God has kept His promises to them, merely because He acts redemptively toward others. (Matthew 20:11.) The Lord reproved those who worked in His service for resenting the fact that the same salvational wages would be paid to those who came late. He asked, "Is thine eye evil, because I am good?" (Matthew 20:15.) We worship a generous God who desires us to be generous like Him.

Meekness is careful regarding its expectations of others. Those who are unmeek often expect more of others than they do of themselves. They are sometimes angry when disappointed by those around them, including leaders. They are not as willing to "give place" for others to grow. The tendency is to pull down, rather than to lift up. Rigidity is there instead of gentleness, and the tendency to make demands instead of graciousness.

The meek are glad to "give place" for others to grow; in their patience, they also give time. Therefore, far from wishing to dominate others, they rejoice when others grow, and their rejoicing is as genuine as their giving place and time.

When we are thus settled, we will be less eager to murmur, to complain, or to steady the ark. Indeed, one of the great risks of murmuring is that we can become too efficient at it, too puffed up, too clever. We can even acquire too large an audience. Alas, what may for some be transitory murmuring may end up, for others, being a springboard that flings them clear out of the Church.

The meek are not concerned with prideful preeminence, including considerations of scale. They are not exercised, for instance, over quantitative considerations with regard to the comparative lack of size of God's chosen people. The Lord put that concern to rest centuries ago when He told the Israelites:

> Thou art an holy people unto the Lord thy God: the Lord thy God hath chosen thee to be a special people unto himself, above all people that are upon the face of the earth.
>
> The Lord did not set his love upon you, nor choose you, because ye were more in number than any people; for ye were the fewest of all people: But because the Lord loved you, and because he would keep the oath which he had sworn unto your fathers, hath the Lord brought you out with a mighty hand, and redeemed you out of the house of bondmen, from the hand of Pharaoh king of Egypt.
>
> Know therefore that the Lord thy God, he is God, the faithful God, which keepeth covenant and mercy with them that love him and keep his commandments to a thousand generations. (Deuteronomy 7:6–9.)

The Church will be much larger in the latter days than it now is, as we learn from prophecy. (D&C 105:31.)

Nevertheless, the Church's "dominions upon the face of the earth" will still be comparatively small. Its members will be "scattered upon all the face of the earth," but it will still not be demographically dominant. (1 Nephi 14:12, 14.) The people of the Lord, therefore, have a sense of destiny but also an almost amusing unconcern with scale. Jacob declared: "Now, my beloved brethren, seeing that our merciful God has given us so great knowledge concerning these things, let us remember him, and lay aside our sins, and not hang down our heads, for we are not cast off; nevertheless, we have been driven out of the land of our inheritance; but we have been led to a better land, for the Lord has made the sea our path, and we are upon an isle of the sea." (2 Nephi 10:20.) Either North or South America is a big island! So much for considerations of scale.

Pride, not meekness, leads to exclusionary hobbies within the Church or the gospel. Hobbies can give an individual a sense of preeminence, a cause to be lifted up. There are those in the Church, unfortunately, who like such an edge. Some such persons resist counsel concerning how they are missing the balancing dimensions of the gospel. Having conscientiously and effectively pursued a particular doctrine or portion of the gospel, they may, in fact, have unusual knowledge in that particular thing. (Alma 32:34.) For them, however, the incremental process of verification stops, and what has been acquired becomes a coveted source of pride.

The meek, on the other hand, are quick to move on in the process of validation and excitement over each successive gospel principle or experience. They know there is more than one flower in the gospel garden, and they are not reclusive or possessive about some edge they might have. Meek individuals know they are set apart to serve, not merely set apart to observe. It is the proud, not the meek, who keep score. The meek are not playing games for those in the grandstand.

The meek are slow to judge, whereas the proud are quick, even eager to judge. The meek will not withhold compassion or help, saying that "the man has brought upon himself his misery." (Mosiah 4:17.) Even though the individual may have done just that, they are nevertheless slow to judge. Being more open to the truth, the meek are more free, while the proud are compassed about with the glitzed self-sufficiency that keeps them from grasping the hand of fellowship extended to all by the Lord's prophets.

As we speak of the importance of meekness in the process of learning, it is not necessary to distinguish overmuch between secular learning and spiritual learning: however, the larger the issues, the more meekness matters. Paul complained of those who were "ever learning, and never able to come to the knowledge of the truth." (2 Timothy 3:7.) The Moffatt Version renders those same words "always curious to learn and never able to attain the knowledge of the truth." Furthermore, in the Moffatt Version, such individuals are described as "hostile to the truth." The Revised Standard Version describes individuals "who will listen to anybody and can never arrive at a knowledge of the truth" as individuals who have a "counterfeit faith."

Meekness creates the ultimate openness, the openness to spiritual things. Of course, the work-horse way of learning—secular and spiritual—is by experience. As Laban said to Jacob in ancient Israel, "I have learned by experience that the Lord hath blessed me for thy sake." (Genesis 30:27.) Nor is spiritual learning automatically at odds with secular learning; it simply goes beyond. "Moses was learned in all the wisdom of the Egyptians, and was mighty in words and in deeds." (Acts 7:22.)

The truly meek individual combines realism and love. He recognizes that spiritual growth requires voluntary cooperation with God; "there is no other way," just as there is "none other name under heaven, given among men, whereby we must be saved." (Acts 4:12.) Love in that meek person will give place for such a process to occur.

Whether the moment involves "What think ye of Christ?" or "Whom say ye that I am?" (Matthew 22:42; 16:15), the meek person will not resort to stampeding, pushing, and provoking. Agency and process are both respected.

Such persons learn the feelings that underlay the lamentation "O Jerusalem..." or those that underlay the observation "I have not found so great faith, no, not in all Israel." (Matthew 23:37; 8:10.) Meekness underwrites the long-suffering and patience. Did not Amulek say that he had been "called many times and... would not hear"? (Alma 10:6.) The meek are willing to patiently serve, to "work the crowd," those who comprise the "multitudes in the valley of decision." (Joel 3:14.)

By combining realism and love, the meek know those great rejoicing moments when others have "chosen the good part." The resurrected Jesus wept twice in the course of blessing children in Bountiful. (3 Nephi 17:21-22.) Those who are meek are also unthreatened in their own commitment merely because others do not make that same commitment.

After the death of the Prophet Joseph Smith, some thought that large numbers would follow Sidney Rigdon. Of this possibility Brigham Young confidently but meekly said, "All I ask of men or women to do, is, if they believe in Sidney Rigdon and want him to lead them, I want they should be bold enough to go with him."[15]

NOTES

1. Henry Fairlie, *The Seven Deadly Sins Today,* p. 39.
2. *Interpreter's Dictionary of the Bible,* p. 876.
3. Fairlie, p. 40.
4. Ibid., p. 45.
5. Ibid., p. 42.

6. Ibid., p. 43.
7. Ibid., p. 51.
8. *Journal of Discourses* 11:252.
9. Joseph Smith, *History of the Church* 2:23.
10. *Teachings of the Prophet Joseph Smith,* p. 181.
11. *Journal of Discourses* 5:55–56.
12. Harold B. Lee, *Stand Ye in Holy Places,* p. 346.
13. Joseph Smith, *History of the Church* 6:314.
14. Alan Hayward, *God Is,* p. 68.
15. *Times and Seasons* 5:667.

Chapter Five

THE GRACE
OF GOD

"My grace is sufficient for the meek;... if men come
unto me I will show unto them their weakness. I give
unto men weakness that they may be humble; and
my grace is sufficient for all men that humble themselves before me." (Ether 12:26–27)

When the Lord declared, "My sheep hear my voice, ...
and they follow me" (John 10:27), it was not only an
indication that a profound process of recognition and
familiarity would be at work; it also bespoke the role of
operational meekness—listening long and humbly enough
for the recognition to occur. This readiness, with ears to
hear, has been needed in all dispensations but never more
than after the Restoration. The restitution of all things
ended centuries of deprivation, but it also goes sharply
against the grain of heedless secular societies. So while
the truths of the restoration would be had again, they
would be useful only "among as many as shall believe."
(Moses 1:41.) Yet those astray include "a few humble
followers of Christ" who, in some instances, only "err
because they are taught by the precepts of men." (2 Nephi
28:14.) In fact, the adversary's kingdom "must shake" in
order that those who will may be "stirred up unto
repentance." (2 Nephi 28:19.)

The importance of the meekness factor is evident both
in accepting the gospel and in observing it in purity and
simplicity. We understand why Jesus chose humble
Galilean fishermen. Otherwise, as George MacDonald
declared, we would have "had a system founded on a
human interpretation of the divine gospel, instead of the
gospel itself."[1] In fact, not long after the fishermen were
gone, that is exactly what began to occur regarding
certain truths and ordinances.

How much we are able to perceive in the first place and how we then regard it depend upon our degree of humbleness of mind. George MacDonald observed, "Meekness alone makes the spiritual retina pure to receive God's things as they are."[2] Indeed, the Spirit does teach us the transcending truths "of things as they really are, and of things as they really will be" (Jacob 4:13) and likewise gives us "knowledge of things...as they were" (D&C 93:24). The truth about such realities constitutes what Paul called the "deep things of God." (1 Corinthians 2:10.)

Intellectual stubbornness, on the other hand, can bring about such sad situations. In Jacob we read: "Behold, the Jews were a stiffnecked people; and they despised the words of plainness, and killed the prophets, and sought for things that they could not understand. Wherefore, because of their blindness, which blindness came by looking beyond the mark, they must needs fall; for God hath taken away his plainness from them, and delivered unto them many things which they cannot understand, because they desired it. And because they desired it God hath done it, that they may stumble." (Jacob 4:14.)

An angel advised Nephi that other books would come forth that would make known certain plain and precious things that had been taken away. (1 Nephi 13:40.) After all, Jesus' criticism of the religious establishments of His time included their having, in effect, taken away the key of knowledge. In the Joseph Smith translation of Luke 11:53, the key of knowledge is defined as "the fullness of the scriptures." Blessed are the meek who received the growing completeness of the scriptures ushered in by the Restoration.

When Jesus taught the people that Moses had prophesied about Him (John 5:46), it was not sufficiently persuasive for most people at that time who had a far different mind-set. Those like Philip saw the connection, but few others. (John 1:45.)

Thus, the other books of scriptures that came forth through the Prophet Joseph Smith are to play an unusual role: they will be needed to convince some that the Bible, "the records of the prophets and the twelve apostles," is true. (1 Nephi 13:39.) Through this restoration process, plain and precious things that had been kept back and taken away would be—to use the words of the Lord to Moses—"had again" among the believing children of men! Only those with humbleness of mind would welcome the restored scriptures, however.

Because the plain and precious parts of the gospel were "kept back" (1 Nephi 13:34), this has caused some in the gentile nations to "stumble exceedingly." What was missing would cause tremendous difficulties, with resultant mind-sets to be overcome only where there is sufficient humbleness of mind.

Unsurprisingly, the revelation received by the Prophet Joseph Smith in June 1830, which we now know as the first chapter of the Book of Moses, was totally consistent with what Joseph had translated a year or so earlier in the thirteenth chapter of First Nephi. Moses was advised by the Lord that in a day when people of the earth would "esteem [the Lord's] words as naught," and following the period when many of the things Moses would write would be taken from the book, the Lord would, in the latter days, raise up one "like unto" Moses so that these precious truths would be "had again." (Moses 1:41.)

Key truths were included in the revelations to Moses that were not carried forward, causing people to "stumble exceedingly." Among these was the fact that Moses "saw God face to face" (Moses 1:2), not merely his "back parts" (Exodus 33:23).

Moses was further advised that he was in the similitude of Jehovah-Jesus. (Moses 1:6.) This is a major matter inasmuch as certain scholars, then and now, emphasize an immaterial god, shunning anything anthropomorphic.[3] The role of Adam as the first man was likewise verified in the Lord's discussion with Moses. (Moses 1:34.)

Moreover, Moses saw the workmanship of God regarding this planet and its inhabitants (Moses 1:4), coming to know, unlike provincial Laman and Lemuel, "the dealings of that God who had created them." (1 Nephi 2:12. See also Mosiah 10:14.)

Moses learned that God knew all things, because all things were present with God. (Moses 1:6.) Furthermore, there was a plurality of worlds, for God had created other worlds without number. (Moses 1:33.) The underlying purpose of this planet, and presumably of other worlds, was summationally stated by the Lord, who said, to an inquiring Moses ("Tell me, ... why these things are so?"), "This is my work and my glory—to bring to pass the immortality and eternal life of man." (Moses 1:30, 39.)

These stretching truths are part of the fundamental framework of faith. Without them, mortals can stray and stumble exceedingly, whether out of puzzlement or wonderment. Some become mistaken as to whether or not this is an explainable world. Others are befuddled as to the nature and purpose of God and whether we are, in fact, really created in His image. Still others are uncertain and undecided concerning Christ. So there was (and is) "a division among the people because of him." (John 7:43.) There are many other ways in which the spiritually uninformed "stumble exceedingly," especially as to the "great question." Note the clarity of one prophecy as to Jesus yet to come and His statement to the Nephites when he introduced Himself: "He shall be called Jesus Christ, the Son of God, the Father of heaven and earth, the Creator of all things from the beginning." (Mosiah 3:8.) "Behold, I am Jesus Christ the Son of God. I created the heavens and the earth, and all things that in them are. I was with the Father from the beginning." (3 Nephi 9:15.)

The reality as to the nature of God is so basic, as the Prophet Joseph Smith declared: "The great majority of mankind do not comprehend anything, either that which is past, or that which is to come, as it respects their relationship to God. They do not know, neither do they understand the nature of that relationship.... If men do not comprehend the character of God, they do not comprehend themselves."[4]

No wonder there was both prior and later satanic resistance, in Moses' time as well as in Joseph Smith's time, in view of the priority and urgency of the truths that were to flow through these men concerning the dealings of God with mankind. As we are told by Alma, "all the dealings of the Lord" are merciful and verified. (Alma 50:19.) Such cannot be known unless we understand God's plans and are meek enough to comply with them.

Not only do the meek see these basic truths, but they also begin to understand better the utterances of Jesus of Nazareth that otherwise might be viewed as imagery instead of theology.

One episode is illustrative as to how much more there is to contemplate, if we have humbleness of mind and savor the fullness of the gospel:

O ye people of these great cities which have fallen, who are descendants of Jacob, yea, who are of the house of Israel, how oft have I gathered you as a hen gathereth her chickens under her wings, and have nourished you.

And again, how oft would I have gathered you as a hen gathereth her chickens under her wings,

O Jerusalem, Jerusalem, thou that killest the prophets, and stonest them which are sent unto thee, how often would I have gathered thy children together, even as a hen gathereth her chickens under her wings, and ye would not!

Behold, your house is left unto you desolate. (Matthew 23:37-38.)

yea, O ye people of the house of Israel, ... ye that dwell at Jerusalem, as ye that have fallen; yea how oft would I have gathered you as a hen gathereth her chickens, and ye would not.

O ye house of Israel whom I have spared, how oft will I gather you as a hen gathereth her chickens under her wings, if ye will repent and return unto me with full purpose of heart. (3 Nephi 10:4-6.)

Who will gather his people even as a hen gathereth her chickens under her wings, even as many as will hearken to my voice and humble themselves before me, and call upon me in mighty prayer. (D&C 29:2.)

This Lordly lamentation not only showed clearly that Jesus was Jehovah, but still more is involved, as we learn from a modern Prophet:

President Joseph Smith ... took for the foundation of his discourse the words of Jesus to the Jews, "how often would I have gathered thy children together, even as a hen gathereth her chickens under her wings, and ye would not," etc. He then asked what was the object of gathering the Jews together or the people of God in any age of the world. The main object was to build unto the Lord an house whereby he could reveal unto his people the ordinances of his house and glories of his kingdom and teach the people the ways of salvation, for there are certain ordinances and principles that, when they are taught and practiced, must be done in a place built for that purpose. This was purposed in the mind of God before the world was and it was for this purpose that God designed to gather together the Jews oft but they would not.

It is for the same purpose that God gathers together the people in the last days to build unto the Lord an house to prepare them for ordinances and endowments, washings and anointings, etc. One of the ordinances of the house of the Lord is baptism for the dead. God decreed before the foundation of the world that that ordinance should be administered in a house prepared for that purpose. If a man gets the fulness of God, he has to get [it] in the same way that Jesus Christ obtain[ed] it, and that was by keeping all the ordinances of the house of the Lord.[5]

More than we know, the connection is there between all ages and races, indeed, "the whole human family of Adam." (Mormon 3:20.) The gospel has been common to each dispensation in one degree or another. (Moses 5:58–59.) As Jacob wrote, "For this intent have we written these things, that they [our children] may know that we knew of Christ, and we had a hope of his glory many hundred years before his coming; and not only we ourselves had a hope of his glory, but also all the holy prophets which were before us." (Jacob 4:4.)

Meekness is so necessary as to our readiness to learn not only these sweeping truths but particular truths as well, which come incrementally, "line upon line, precept upon precept." (D&C 98:12.) The Prophet Joseph Smith, for instance, first translated the thirteenth chapter of First Nephi in perhaps late 1828 or the spring of 1829. These verses note that certain things had been "kept back" and "taken away." In June 1830, Joseph received the "precious morsel" we know as the first chapter of Moses. Therein Moses was told by the Lord that of the scriptures Moses would write, certain individuals would "take many of them from the book." (Moses 1:41.) It was not until February 16, 1832, however, after a conference in Amherst, Ohio, that Joseph said it was apparent to him, "from sundry revelations which had been received," that "many important points touching the salvation of man had been taken from the Bible, or lost before it was compiled." (Preface to D&C 76.) On that date, among other things, came the sunburst of celestial truths about the three degrees of glory.

Only as Joseph, in humbleness of mind, began to work with and search and ponder the scriptures did he begin to sense fully that things were missing and also how significant some omissions were. The glorious revelation of that February day is a stunning example of how Joseph's readiness met God's graciousness.

With regard to the idea of differential divine disclosure, how anxious the Prophet was to impart more of what he had been given by God: "It is my meditation all the day & more than my meat & drink to know how I shall make the saints of God to comprehend the visions that roll like an overflowing surge, before my mind."[6]

"I could explain a hundred fold more than I ever have of the glories of the kingdoms manifested to me in the vision, were I permitted, and were the people prepared to receive them. The Lord deals with this people as a tender parent with a child, communicating light and intelligence and the knowledge of his ways as they can bear it."[7]

The absence of meekness on our part not only results in a lack of readiness to receive more from the Lord and His prophets, but it can also cause impatience to know before we are ready. Alma tells us: "It is given unto many to know the mysteries of God; nevertheless they are laid under a strict command that they shall not impart only according to the portion of his word which he doth grant unto the children of men, according to the heed and diligence which they give unto him." (Alma 12:9.)

There is a grand scheme in which the Light of the world provides as much illumination as is appropriate in His wisdom: "For behold, the Lord doth grant unto all nations, of their own nation and tongue, to teach his word, yea, in wisdom, all that he seeth fit that they should have; therefore we see that the Lord doth counsel in wisdom, according to that which is just and true." (Alma 29:8.)

Thus we are to be appreciative as well as patient regarding further unfolding. After the resurrected Jesus had taught the Nephites, Mormon wrote: "And when

they [the Nephites] shall have received this, which is
expedient that they should have first, to try their faith,
and if it shall so be that they shall believe these things
then shall the greater things be made manifest unto
them. And if it so be that they will not believe these
things, then shall the greater things be withheld from
them, unto their condemnation. Behold, I was about to
write them, all which were engraven upon the plates of
Nephi, but the Lord forbade it, saying: I will try the faith
of my people." (3 Nephi 26:9-11.)

The meek are grateful for all Divine disclosures,
however humble and obscure the surrounding circumstances. On May 3, 1842, Joseph Smith recorded the
following:

> I spent the day in the upper part of the store, that is in my
> private office...in council with General James Adams, of
> Springfield, Patriarch Hyrum Smith, Bishops Newel K.
> Whitney and George Miller, and President Brigham Young
> and Elders Heber C. Kimball and Willard Richards, instructing
> them in the principles and order of the Priesthood, attending
> to washings, anointings, endowments and the communication
> of keys pertaining to the Aaronic Priesthood, and so on to the
> highest order of the Melchizedek Priesthood, setting forth the
> order pertaining to the Ancient of Days, and all those plans
> and principles by which any one is enabled to secure the
> fullness of those blessings which have been prepared for the
> Church of the First Born, and come up and abide in the
> presence of the Eloheim in the eternal worlds. In this council
> was instituted the ancient order of things for the first time in
> these last days. And the communications I made to this
> council were of things spiritual, and to be received only by
> the spiritual minded: and there was nothing made known to
> these men but what will be made known to all the Saints of
> the last days, so soon as they are prepared to receive, and a
> proper place is prepared to communicate them, even to the
> weakest of the Saints; therefore let the Saints be diligent in
> building the Temple, and all houses which they have been, or
> shall hereafter be, commanded of God to build; and wait their

time with patience in all meekness, faith, perseverance unto the end, knowing assuredly that all these things referred to in this council are always governed by the principle of revelation.[8]

Joseph Smith was very conscious of not only the revelations that had come to him, but also the time frame. In one of his closing sermons, the King Follett sermon given April 7, 1844, he spoke about "the revelation that I have [been] given the last 16 years."[9] The revelations to be codified commenced in 1828, sixteen years earlier, with what we now have as sections 3 and 10 of the Doctrine and Covenants.

Meekness helps us to surmount the stumbling blocks so that we are prepared to receive a deeper and wider view. Obviously, Philip had such meekness when he recognized Jesus as the Messiah of whom Moses had spoken. (John 1:45.) Obviously, Paul had the broad view when he described Moses as having, by choice, forgone life in Pharaoh's court for a life of service to Jesus. (Hebrews 11:24–27.) Nevertheless, the stones of stumbling are real. In fact, these offending rocks prove insurmountable unless we have the attribute of meekness.

In our own time, Joseph Smith, the First Vision, and the Book of Mormon constitute stumbling blocks for many—around or over which they cannot get—unless they are meek enough to examine all the evidence at hand, not being exclusionary as a result of accumulated attitudes in a secular society. Humbleness of mind is the initiator of expansiveness of mind.

It is ironic that many in Jesus' time refused to listen to Him because they were so fixed on Moses. To those who persecuted Him because He had healed an invalid on the Sabbath, he said: "Had ye believed Moses, ye would have believed me: for he wrote of me. But if ye believe not his writings, how shall ye believe my words?" (John 5:46–47. See also Mormon 7:9.)

Yet Jesus had personally called, instructed, and tutored Moses! He told the Nephites, "Behold, ... the law is fulfilled that was given unto Moses. Behold, I am he that gave the law, and I am he who covenanted with my people Israel; therefore, the law in me is fulfilled, for I have come to fulfill the law; therefore it hath an end." (3 Nephi 15:4–5.)

Likewise in our time, people are slow to see the significant parallels between Jesus' two meek servants—two meek men—Moses and Joseph Smith, Jr. The Lord declared that the restoring, latter-day prophet would be "like unto" Moses: "And in a day when the children of men shall esteem my words as naught and take many of them from the book which thou shalt write, behold, I will raise up another *like unto thee;* and they shall be had again among the children of men—among as many as shall believe." (Moses 1:41; italics added. See also 2 Nephi 3:9.) Thus, when certain truths of the gospel were to be "had again among the children of men," it would be through a meek one whom God would raise up and who would be like unto meek Moses.

Without striving overmuch to produce exact parallels, certain parallels are nevertheless worth noting, as between Moses and Joseph Smith.

The exceedingly high mountain on which Moses conversed with the Lord was probably associated with his "middle" life spent in the Sinai. This was likely *after* the burning bush but *before* Israel's exodus from Egypt. On this occasion, Moses had a terrifying encounter with Satan, and he "began to fear exceedingly." (Moses 1:20.) Moses' remarkable spiritual experience did not come unaccompanied by a traumatic encounter with the adversary. In the Sacred Grove Joseph Smith experienced the power of the adversary; it was "an astonishing influence." The darkness was thick, Joseph said, and for a time he felt "doomed to sudden destruction." (JS-H 1:15–16.)

Both Moses and Joseph experienced "face to face" meetings with the Lord. (Moses 1:2; JS-H 1:17-18.) Both were exhausted by the experience. (Moses 1:9-11; JS-H 1:20.)

Both ancient Moses and modern Joseph prepared their people to journey to respective promised lands, but they were not themselves permitted to enter therein. (Deuteronomy 3:27; 34:6; Alma 45:19; D&C 135.)

Both Moses and Joseph were libeled and slandered, including accusations that they were power hungry and that they misused authority and paid too little heed to their "lieutenants," some of whom were quick to accuse.

Moses' challenges also came from within his inner circle, including at one point Miriam and Aaron, who "spake against Moses because of the Ethiopian woman whom he had married.... And they said, Hath the Lord indeed spoken only by Moses? hath he not spoken also by us? And the Lord heard it." (Numbers 12:1-2.)

Moses had a challenge on a larger scale. Dathan and 250 prestigious leaders once confronted him: "And they rose up before Moses, with certain of the children of Israel, two hundred and fifty princes of the assembly, famous in the congregation, men of renown: and they gathered themselves together against Moses and against Aaron, and said unto them, Ye take too much upon you, seeing all the congregation are holy, every one of them, and the Lord is among them: wherefore then lift ye up yourselves above the congregation of the Lord?...Is it a small thing that thou hast brought us up out of a land that floweth with milk and honey, to kill us in the wilderness, except thou make thyself altogether a prince over us?" (Numbers 16:2-3, 13.)

Joseph Smith, too, endured major defections from the inner circle in Kirtland, in Missouri, and, still later, in Nauvoo, being said by some to be a fallen prophet.

Both prophets were in the process of developing and leading a group known as Israel—ancient and modern.

Both were required to lead a people who were a "mixed multitude." (Exodus 12:38.)

Both prophets were accused of poor planning, which was alleged to have caused people to be miserable whether in the Sinai or in the Zion's Camp march. The children of Israel complained to Moses, "Is not this the word that we did tell thee in Egypt, saying, Let us alone, that we may serve the Egyptians? For it had been better for us to serve the Egyptians, than that we should die in the wilderness." (Exodus 14:12.) Later they murmured against Moses and Aaron, saying: "Would to God we had died by the hand of the Lord in the land of Egypt, when we sat by the flesh pots, and when we did eat bread to the full; for ye have brought us forth into this wilderness, to kill this whole assembly with hunger." (Exodus 16:3.) Nephi recounted to his brothers the history of Israel, explaining: "And notwithstanding they being led, the Lord their God, their Redeemer, going before them, leading them by day and giving light unto them by night, and doing all things for them which were expedient for man to receive, they hardened their hearts and blinded their minds, and reviled against Moses and against the true and living God." (1 Nephi 17:30.)

Both men had questions raised about marital decisions they had made: Moses with regard to the Cushite or Ethiopian woman (Numbers 12:1-2), and Joseph in connection with the revelations concerning plural marriage.

Though Joseph Smith appears to have been less victimized by people's wondering why they were being led from situations of comfort into comparative misery, both men experienced the voicing of this challenge from at least some of their followers.

In Moses' case, he was asked several times why he brought the people to the wilderness to suffer; some of them even wished they could return to Egypt, where they were at least cared for as slaves. (Exodus 14:12; 16:3.)

"We remember the fish, which we did eat in Egypt freely; the cucumbers, and the melons, and the leeks, and the onions, and the garlick: but now our soul is dried away: there is nothing at all, beside this manna, before our eyes." (Numbers 11:5-6.) "And they journeyed from mount Hor by the way of the Red sea, to compass the land of Edom: and the soul of the people was much discouraged because of the way. And the people spake against God, and against Moses, Wherefore have ye brought us up out of Egypt to die in the wilderness? for there is no bread, neither is there any water; and our soul loatheth this light bread. And the Lord sent fiery serpents among the people, and they bit the people; and much people of Israel died." (Numbers 21:4-6.) The same attitude of disaffected followership was reflected in Nephi's exodus. (1 Nephi 17:20.)

Both Moses and Joseph received—perhaps required—reassuring and reinforcing spiritual experiences after the time of their initial call.

Both prophets, at certain points in their ministry, utilized spokesmen: Aaron for Moses (Exodus 4:27, 30), and Oliver Cowdery and Sidney Rigdon at various and earlier times for Joseph Smith. Yet both were less than perfect.

Both prophets knew what it was to be let down by those upon whom they should have been able to count: Moses in the case of Aaron and the golden calf (Exodus 32), and Joseph with defections from the First Presidency and the Twelve.

Both, in a sense, were drafted by the Lord. They did not start out seeking to become prophets. Moses was surprised by the episode of the burning bush. Joseph Smith was merely trying to find out which of many churches he was to join; it had not occurred to him that all were wrong. (JS-H 1:18.) For Joseph, it started out as simply a question of affiliation. Instead, Joseph launched a dispensation!

Both prophets provided us with added books of scripture and revelation. Modern Joseph brought back some of the truths that had been held back or taken away from what Moses had written, as commanded.

Both of them were thrust into entirely new situations and came to know the fatigue and loneliness of leadership. Hence these lamentations from Moses: "Ye have been rebellious against the Lord from the day that I knew you." (Deuteronomy 9:24.) "I am not able to bear all this people alone, because it is too heavy for me." (Numbers 11:14.) A beleaguered Joseph, a Joseph who already knew more than he could tell, pleaded: "Why will not man learn Wisdom by precept & example at this late age of the world & not be obliged to learn every thing we know by sad experience?" [10]

Both men wished to share more of the leadership burdens with their spiritually enlightened people and followers. Moses told Joshua, "Enviest thou for my sake? would God that all the Lord's people were prophets, and that the Lord would put his spirit upon them!" (Numbers 11:29.) Through Joseph Smith, the Lord said: "But that every man might speak in the name of God the Lord, even the Savior of the world." (D&C 1:20.)

Both men developed greater mercy and empathy as a result of their adversity. Moses asked the Lord, "Why doth thy wrath wax hot against thy people, which thou hast brought forth out of the land of Egypt with great power, and with a mighty hand? Wherefore should the Egyptians speak, and say, For mischief did he bring them out, to slay them in the mountains, and to consume them from the face of the earth? Turn from thy fierce wrath... against thy people." (Exodus 32:11-12.) Joseph wrote from Liberty Jail, "It seems to me that my heart will always be more tender after this than ever it was before."[11]

Both were tutored with special tenderness.

In these and other ways there are striking parallels,

just as there are parallels between modern Joseph and ancient Joseph. Even so, the significance is not to be seen solely in the parallels but in the substance of the work done, a work that would have been impossible without their humbleness of mind. Meekness calls forth the vital grace of God, which is one reason the meek are so bounteously blessed.

NOTES

1. George MacDonald, *Life Essential,* p. 69,
2. Ibid., p. 45.
3. Professor R. K. Harrison, in his *Introduction to the Old Testament,* noted one example of an early Jewish convert "attempting to remove many of the Old Testament anthropomorphic expressions." Professor Harrison described as well how Hebrew originals were interpreted by translators who "showed no scruples about interpreting the text to make it conform to their own theological predictions." (Pp. 234, 232.)
4. *Teachings of the Prophet Joseph Smith,* p. 343.
5. Andrew F. Ehat and Lyndon W. Cook, eds., *The Words of Joseph Smith,* pp. 212-13. This quotation is from the diary of Wilford Woodruff, and the spelling has been modernized and punctuation added. See also *History of the Church* 5:423.
6. *The Words of Joseph Smith,* p. 196. See also *History of the Church* 5:362.
7. *History of the Church* 5:402.
8. Ibid., 5:1-2.
9. *The Words of Joseph Smith,* p. 351.
10. *The Words of Joseph Smith,* p. 7. This excerpt is from the Wilford Woodruff diary, and misspellings have been corrected. See also *History of the Church* 3:384.
11. Dean C. Jessee, ed., *The Personal Writings of Joseph Smith,* p. 386.

Chapter Six

BLESSED ARE
THE MEEK

"The meek shall inherit the earth; and shall delight
themselves in an abundance of peace." (Psalm 37:11)

We are told that Aristotle thought meekness was a
very useful golden mean between irascibility and
sluggishness, helping people to maintain their equanimity
and their composure.[1] True as this may be, meekness is so
much more. It also has to do with things of everlasting
and salvational significance. "God arose ... to save all the
meek of the earth." (Psalm 76:9.)

A splendid completeness of character flows from
meekness. Alma taught: "And now I would that ye should
be humble, and be submissive and gentle; easy to be
entreated; full of patience and long-suffering; being
temperate in all things; being diligent in keeping the
commandments of God at all times; asking for whatsoever
things ye stand in need, both spiritual and temporal;
always returning thanks unto God for whatsoever things
ye do receive." (Alma 7:23.)

Moreover, the truly humble individual is eventually
seen by thoughtful peers as possessing genuine and
impressive inner strength. Such observers realize that the
meek individual is not only nice, but also has the special
strength of certitude. This certitude will be evident in the
meek person's communications, as in Peter's prescrip-
tiveness about the need for articulate discipleship:
"Sanctify the Lord God in your hearts: and be ready
always to give an answer to every man that asketh you a
reason of the hope that is in you with meekness and rear."
(1 Peter 3:15.)

The truth may be resented at any time, especially by the proud. But the truth will be resented less when the messenger is meek, as the apostle indicated. Furthermore, declaring and articulating Jesus' gospel is another way of learning of Him. (D&C 32:1.) This same certitude will bring what Paul urged us to have: the gentleness and meekness of Christ. (2 Corinthians 10:1.) In Paul's epistle to Titus, gentleness and courtesy are urged. (Titus 3:2.)

Even if as a benefit meekness stood alone, one reason for developing greater meekness is to have greater access to the grace of God. The Lord guarantees that His grace is sufficient for the meek. (Ether 12:26.) Besides, only the meek know how to know fully his help and assistance.

Meekness, nevertheless, comes trailing a cloud of other beneficial considerations. The prophet Mormon observed that without meekness, there can be no faith nor hope nor love. (Moroni 7:37-47.) Furthermore, remission of our sins brings additional meekness along with the great gift of the Holy Ghost, the Comforter. (Moroni 8:26.) These supernal blessings are not to be enjoyed for any length of time except by those who are meek. But of the joys of the gospel, it has been rightly said, "None receiveth save it be the truly penitent and humble seeker of happiness." (Alma 27:18.)

Furthermore, we cannot even have faith, except we be meek and lowly in heart. (Moroni 7:43-45.) Thus we are able to enjoy greater faith, hope, love, knowledge, and reassurance. We will know the answer to the "great question," for it is by the power of the Holy Ghost that we know that Jesus is the Christ. Thus the meek receive the great answers and the great blessings.

Remarkable blessings do depend upon the presence of several virtues, and surely meekness is among them; having it affects not only eternity but also daily life: "The meek shall eat and be satisfied." "The meek will he guide in judgment: and the meek will he teach his way." (Psalms 22:26; 25:9.)

In contrast to meekness, of course, are generic grief-causers, such as aggressiveness, coarseness, selfishness, and all forms of insensitivity.

The perils of "puffery" are especially real when combined with iniquity: "O the wise, and the learned, and the rich, that are puffed up in the pride of their hearts, and all those who preach false doctrines, and all those who commit whoredoms, and pervert the right way of the Lord, wo, wo, wo be unto them, saith the Lord God Almighty, for they shall be thrust down to hell!" (2 Nephi 28:15.) Those who are puffed up need constantly to be reinflated, hence the tendency of some to "play to the galleries," including by way of criticism of the kingdom.

Being *in* the world but not being *of* the world sets apart the serious, meek disciple not only in viewpoint but also in lifestyle. Paul admonished the followers of Christ "to speak evil of no man, to be no brawlers, but gentle, shewing all meekness unto all men." (Titus 3:1.) "Now I Paul myself beseech you by the meekness and gentleness of Christ, who in presence am base among you, but being absent am gold toward you." (2 Corinthians 10:1.) John declared: "For all that is in the world, the lust of the flesh, and the lust of the eyes, and the pride of life, is not of the Father, but is of the world." (1 John 2:16.)

Heavenly power can be accessed only by those who are Christlike; it is a power whose continued availability is maintained by meekness along with the other virtues. Nor can we have the loving empathy or understanding mercy necessary for true discipleship without meekness. Paul taught: "Thou, O man of God, ... follow after righteousness, godliness, faith, love, patience, meekness." (1 Timothy 6:11.) In King Benjamin's address, we read that a saint "becometh as a child, submissive, meek, humble, patient, full of love, willing to submit to all things which the Lord seeth fit to inflict upon him, even as a child doth submit to his father." (Mosiah 3:19.) One of Moses' few relapses involved a brief lack of meekness: "And Moses and Aaron gathered the congregation together before the rock, and he said unto them, Hear now, ye rebels; must we fetch you water out of this rock?" (Numbers 20:10.)

Naaman, the military commander, who was very familiar with status and authority and who was accustomed to being obeyed, nevertheless proved open to feedback even when it was given to him by his orderlies and aides de camp. (See 2 Kings 5:8–14.) He was secure. Those less secure are "proud, knowing nothing, but doting about questions and strifes of words, whereof cometh envy, strife, railings, evil surmisings." (1 Timothy 6:4.) Such do not want advice from their orderlies when their pride has been wounded.

Our esteem for others actually depends upon our meekness: "Be of the same mind one toward another. Mind not high things, but condescend to men of low estate. Be not wise in your own conceits." (Romans 12:16.) Self-sufficiency, on the other hand, blocks such regard from those who "are wise in their own eyes, and prudent in their own sight!" (Isaiah 5:21.)

Vital spiritual data are excluded on an almost reflexive basis because of "the vainness, and the frailties, and the foolishness of men! When they are learned they think they are wise, and they hearken not unto the counsel of God, for they set it aside, supposing they know of themselves, wherefore, their wisdom is foolishness and it profiteth them not. And they shall perish." (2 Nephi 9:28.)

True leaders who genuinely love those about them also are good listeners. Among recent Church leaders who have managed power, status, and authority very well was President N. Eldon Tanner. In groups where he could have overwhelmed others with his prestige and abilities, he preferred to let his ideas have a life of their own. Thus he advanced his ideas so that they could be truly tested and received, reflecting the meek and gentle spirit that ornamented that man.

The tendency to crave being praised or being given credit has many disadvantages: for example, if they are not sufficiently praised, some people tend to nurse a grievance until it cankers their souls. There are times when we must be able to forgo recognition and praise as well as able to take criticism or deprivation in order to go on giving.

When we have too much of an investment in the praise, pleasures, and cares of the world, we not only have the attendant difficulties ourselves, but our pride and insensitivity inevitably have an adverse impact on others. The Lord told the people of Jerusalem, "Behold, this was the iniquity of thy sister Sodom, pride, fulness of bread, and abundance of idleness was in her and in her daughters, neither did she strengthen the hand of the poor and needy." (Ezekiel 16:49.)

Not only does our capacity to feel shrink, but we are also shut down intellectually. The sources whence correcting counsel might come are not regarded. Nephi lamented, "And now I, Nephi, cannot say more; the Spirit stoppeth mine utterance, and I am left to mourn because of the unbelief, and the wickedness, and the ignorance, and the stiffneckedness of men; for they will not search knowledge, nor understand great knowledge, when it is given unto them in plainness, even as plain as word can be." (2 Nephi 32:7.)

We all have certain expectations that can be violated by developing circumstances. If we are not meek, the surprise or disappointment incurred by the violation of such expectations can throw us off our stride and even cause us to stumble.

How marvelous when unjust criticism can be managed meekly! This was the case with Brigham Young. For one brief moment, the Prophet Joseph Smith unjustifiably reproved loyal Brigham. Of that brief episode, which involved the transgressions of William Smith, President Lorenzo Snow said, "Brigham Young was equal to the danger" and instantly and meekly yielded to the Prophet. Such was the spiritual significance of that moment, not William's transgressions, for which William was later excommunicated.[2] Years later, John Taylor, then president of the Twelve, yielded similarly to President Brigham Young, who had reproved him concerning a matter pertaining to the United Order.[3] Elder Taylor's prompt and meek visit to President Young saw the two men quickly reconciled. Their being united was more vital than the detail regarding the United Order. How often in human history have lesser men gone unreconciled—to the disadvantage of all concerned?

Since life in the Church presents to us, painfully at times, our own defects as well as the defects of others, we are bound to be disappointed in ourselves and in others. We cannot expect it to be otherwise in a kingdom where not only does the "net gather of every kind," but those of "every kind" are at every stage of spiritual development. (Matthew 13:47.) When people "leave their nets straightway," they come as they are. (See Matthew 4:20.) Though they are already in the initial process of changing, the luggage reflects their past. Hence, this is a developmental journey that requires patience, understanding, and meekness toward others who join the caravan, as, together, we disengage from one world and prepare ourselves for another.

Though it was difficult for Laman and Lemuel to leave Jerusalem, they finally did so under duress. But they never did undertake the real journey, which was that of being each a "man of Christ in a strait and narrow course across that everlasting gulf of misery." (Helaman 3:29.) Since they did not believe that proud and invincible Jerusalem would truly be destroyed, they felt the trip was unnecessary. Their father's colleague, inspired Jeremiah, had nevertheless warned: "Thus saith the Lord, After this manner will I mar the pride of Judah, and the great pride of Jerusalem." (Jeremiah 13:9.) Besides, Laman and Lemuel were being asked to leave comfort and ease for something very different, including when raw meat later appeared on their menu in the wilderness. (1 Nephi 17:2.)

The need for meekness is there in every setting, at every turn, and in every step!

Throughout scripture we encounter the need for us to remember that the Lord has His own timetable for unfolding things; it will not always accord with our schedules or our wants. When, in our extremities, we urgently call for a divine response, there may be, instead, a divine delay. This is not because God, at the moment, is inattentive or loves us less than perfectly. Rather, it is because we are being asked, at the moment, to endure more for the welfare of our souls. The blessed meek understand that God loves them even when they may not be able to explain the meaning of what is happening to them or around them. (1 Nephi 11:17.)

Divine mercy is always operative. It may even cause God to hasten things. Jesus declared, for instance, that except the tribulations of the last days "should be shortened" for the sake of the very elect, no flesh shall be saved. (Matthew 24:22.) When the full heat of the sun comes, "summer is nigh" (Matthew 24:32), and the enveloping events will be blistering.

The Lord can hasten His work "in its time." (D&C 88:73; Isaiah 60:22.) Generally speaking, however, there is a divinely determined pace at which things will move. Even God's revelations come "in their time." (D&C 59:4.) Moreover, though we may wish for swift judgment upon the Lord's enemies, such will not always be dealt out when we might prefer; nevertheless, the Lord's enemies will be "confounded in [His] own due time." (D&C 71:10.) The meek are patient.

If there were too much swiftness, there could be no

long-suffering, no gradual soul stretching, no repenting. With too little time to absorb, to assimilate, and to apply that which has already been given, our capacities would not be fully developed. The developing and the testing of our faith and patience require time. The timing of the Second Coming is not even known by the angels in heaven, an otherwise well-informed group. (Matthew 24:36.)

"For he will give unto the faithful line upon line, precept upon precept; and ... will try you and prove you herewith." (D&C 98:12.) "For behold, thus saith the Lord God: I will give unto the children of men line upon line, precept upon precept, here a little and there a little; and blessed are those who hearken unto my precepts, and lend an ear unto my counsel, for they shall learn wisdom; for unto him that receiveth I will give more; and from them that shall say, We have enough, from them shall be taken away even that which they have." (2 Nephi 28:30.)

It takes time to prepare for eternity.

Furthermore, divine justice requires the record to be clear, so far as our chances for changing are concerned. Even God's enemies are given such opportunities, which are usually rejected at great cost to themselves and others. Everything from stark betrayal to "playing to the galleries" by those seeking the praise of the world will be on the record, indisputably.

Individuals who thus excuse themselves from joy do so by measurable and on-the-record acts of free will. These acts are, alas, demonstrably adverse to their own interests. We are, "according to the flesh," free to choose (2 Nephi 2:27), free to act for ourselves, or we can merely wait passively to be acted upon: "And now remember, remember, my brethren, that whosoever perisheth, perisheth unto himself; and whosoever doeth iniquity, doeth it unto himself; for behold, ye are free; ye are permitted to act for yourselves; for behold, God hath given unto you a knowledge and he hath made you free." (Helaman 14:30. See also 2 Nephi 10:23.)

Even special geographical and political conditions exist for some to maximize their freedom, if such can keep their freedom.

Divine disclosure is metered in "process of time" at a pace largely dependent upon our readiness to receive. Alma explained this to Zeezrom: "It is given unto many to know the mysteries of God; nevertheless they are laid under a strict command that they shall not impart only according to the portion of his word which he doth grant unto the children of men, according to the heed and diligence which they give unto him. And therefore, he that will harden his heart, the same receiveth the lesser portion of the word; and he that will not harden his heart, to him is given the greater portion of the word, until it is given unto him to know the mysteries of God until he know them in full." (Alma 12:9–10.)

So it is that the Lord will both redeem His people and send His wrath upon the earth in His "own due time." (D&C 43:29; 103:2.) However, as noted for His purposes, He may even adjust the times and the seasons. (D&C 121:12; Acts 1:7.) So it is that "all things must come to pass in their own time." (D&C 64:32.) This is cause and reason for patience and perspective amidst the macro plan! Such unfoldingness reflects the tutoring of a just and a long-suffering Lord.

Meanwhile, God desires the record to be crystal clear. Then, in the face of that record, later on we will acknowledge his justice and mercy. (Mosiah 16:1; Alma 12:15.) Besides, we have a notable lack of capacity to appreciate things that, like water out of a fire hydrant, come in a rush. Hence the Lord meters out divine disclosure according to what is deserved and usable. He has warned us: "Murmur not because of the things which thou hast not seen, for they are withheld from thee and from the world, which is wisdom in me in a time to come." (D&C 25:4.) "And when they shall have received this, which is expedient that they should have first, to try their faith, and if it shall so be that they shall believe these things then shall the greater things be made manifest unto them. And if it so be that they will not believe these things, then shall the greater things be withheld from them, unto their condemnation." (3 Nephi 26:9-10.)

Thus, in the process of life, our omniscient Lord has a schedule, a timetable, and a pattern—macro and micro. We all need to know and remember this. Being perfect in His knowledge of us and in His love of us, God is our Perfect Father. The metering and the disclosing by degrees are all part of this mortal process. Therefore, our faith in God includes faith that God lives, faith that He is our Father, and faith that His process (called the plan of salvation) is necessary and proper. But, finally, faith also includes faith in His timetable. Accepting that timetable requires great meekness and patience on our part.

Unlike Jesus in the midst of the agonizing atonement, some of us "shrink" from our bitter cups; we do not meekly and patiently finish our own preparations. (D&C 19:15-19.) Some of us are, in another sense, finished before we are really under way. Others of us are randomly engaged. The Savior characterized such "children of light" as being too casual and as lacking in intensity, compared to the single-minded children of the world. (Luke 16:8.)

Meekness gentles us and tames us so that we are willing to walk resolutely to the edge of the light—where further illumination can occur.

Murmuring, on the other hand, often occurs because of failure to understand doctrines and their implications. Such murmuring usually betrays a lack of meekness. Murmuring can also arise out of a violation of our errant expectations; we then murmur instead of meekly submitting. Contrariwise, those who are willing to submit possess willing hearts and willing minds even when they do not fully comprehend. They display a willingness to wait, reflecting another cardinal virtue—patience. Like our faith, our patience is to be tried as well in order to be developed. (Mosiah 23:21.)

The meek and lowly finally earn this encomium: "And now I would that ye should be humble, and be submissive and gentle; easy to be entreated; full of patience and long-suffering; being temperate in all things; being diligent in keeping the commandments of God at all times; asking for whatsoever things ye stand in need, both spiritual and temporal; always returning thanks unto God for whatsoever things ye do receive." (Alma 7:23.)

The meek are also much less likely to ask amiss in their prayers. (James 4:3.) They are less demanding of life to begin with, hence are less likely to ask selfishly or to act selfishly.

Thus the interplay of individual agency with God's loving purposes for us is greatly facilitated by our meekness. In contrast, to offer ourselves to God, but only as we now are—this is not an acceptable offering. The only individual who might have done that, instead meekly submitted Himself to God's further, shaping will. (Alma 7:11–12.)

Hardheartedness, too, and hearts "set so much upon the things of this world or the honors of men," can be overcome only with more meekness. (D&C 121:35.)

Meekness, by the way, is no stranger to boldness, as noted in the moment of truth between Brigham Young and Sidney Rigdon. A chastened and tutored Peter boldly declared to the crippled man: "Silver and gold have I none; but such as I have give I thee: In the name of the Lord Jesus Christ of Nazareth rise up and walk." (Acts 3:6.)

Meekness is no stranger to healthy self-esteem either. Paul's healthy attitude toward his own past in which he had relentlessly persecuted the Christians was his meek realization that he had been forgiven. He did not intend to let his yesterday hold his tomorrow hostage; instead, he pressed forward and forgot that which was past. (Philippians 3:13–14.)

Practical and spiritual meekness also provides a helpful context for giving and receiving correcting candor when such candor is needed. Graciousness makes easier the following of the injunction of the Lord: "Reproving betimes with sharpness, when moved upon by the Holy Ghost; and then showing forth afterwards an increase of love toward him whom thou hast reproved." (D&C 121:43.) Graciousness facilitates providing the increase in love. President Brigham Young counseled the Saints, "Never chasten beyond the balm you have within you to bind up."[4] Gracious individuals will heed Brigham's counsel. Paul spoke similarly: "Brethren, if a man be overtaken in a fault, ye which are spiritual, restore such an one in the spirit of meekness; considering thyself, lest thou also be tempted." (Galatians 6:1.) Cain was apparently easily offended when his flawed sacrifice was not accepted. (Genesis 4:5; Moses 5:17–23.) Did he expect something else?

The real act of personal sacrifice is not now nor ever has been placing an animal on the altar. Instead, it is a willingness to put the animal that is in us upon the altar—then willingly watching it be consumed! Such is the "sacrifice unto [the Lord of] a broken heart and a contrite spirit." (3 Nephi 9:20.)

Meekness not only dampens our cravings for ascendancy but also helps us avoid needless pique over the ascendancy of others. The brothers of Joseph could not speak peaceably unto him, even though, for all we know, Joseph on his part might have handled sibling relationships better. (Genesis 37:4.) Ultimately, whatever Joseph's imperfections, his brothers were not willing to recognize that the Lord had called their younger brother to special duties.

Meekness could have rescued proud and fearful Judas even after he had left the Last Supper. He could have slipped back in quietly and humbly, rejoining his apostolic colleagues, having belatedly determined not to do the dastardly deed he planned. Meekness can thus rescue us even when we are deep in error. It can rescue us even when others who have written us off will not dare venture into "no man's land" where we lie wounded.

Before he became encrusted with power, Saul knew a time when, Samuel told him, "thou wast little in thine own sight." (1 Samuel 15:17.) Meekness will not stay on as an uninvited guest; it meekly departs where it is not wanted.

David, had he remained meek, would have not slipped into the apparent rationalization that, with the weight of office, he deserved certain privileges. He had reached a point where, apparently, he felt he need not deny himself. Yet the essence of discipleship is, "If any man will come after me, let him deny himself, and take up the cross daily, and follow me." (Luke 9:23.)

What are we to deny ourselves? "It is better that ye should deny yourselves of these things wherein ye will take up your cross, than that ye should be cast into hell." (3 Nephi 12:30.) "These things" in this utterance of Jesus included a recitation of the sensual or selfish. Without such denial, we carry too much baggage. Alas, being overloaded, we then shed not the baggage, but the cross! "Verily I say unto you, Except ye be converted, and become as little children, ye shall not enter into the kingdom of heaven. Whosoever therefore shall humble himself as this little child, the same is greatest in the kingdom of heaven." (Matthew 18:3-4.)

The deserving and blessed meek will not only eventually inherit the earth, they will do so when this planet is really worth inheriting!

Meekness not only enhances spiritual perspective, but it also enlarges souls. Contrariwise, "littleness of soul" (D&C 117:11) insures that only a small view of reality will be taken. One dramatic example of this narrowed view occurred when Cain slew Abel and then gloried and boasted, "I am free." Free? Yes, free to be "a fugitive and a vagabond" in the desert he had made of his own life. Both Cain's desire for Abel's flocks and his being offended at the acceptance of Abel's sacrifice played a part. Proud Cain rejected the greater counsel which was had from God. (Moses 5:25-41.)

The small, myopic view also lends itself to coveting "the drop" while neglecting "the more weighty matters." (D&C 117:8.) In all of our getting and grasping, we do not seem to grasp the implications of this question from the Lord: "Have I not the fowls of heaven, and also the fish of the sea, and the beasts of the mountains? Have I not made the earth? Do I not hold the destinies of all the armies of the nations of the earth?" (D&C 117:6.)

No wonder the Lord also asks us acquisitive mortals, "For what is property unto me?" (D&C 117:4.) "I, the Lord, stretched out the heavens, and built the earth, my very handiwork; and all things therein are mine." (D&C 104:14.)

While we anxiously count pence, the Master measures the mattering moments:

> And being in Bethany in the house of Simon the leper, as he sat at meat, there came a woman having an alabaster box of ointment of spikenard very precious; and she brake the box, and poured it on his head.
>
> And there were some that had indignation within themselves, and said, Why was this waste of the ointment made? For it might have been sold for more than three hundred pence, and have been given to the poor. And they murmured against her.

And Jesus said, Let her alone; why trouble ye her? she hath wrought a good work on me. For ye have the poor with you always, and whensoever ye will ye may do them good: but me ye have not always. She hath done what she could: she is come aforehand to anoint my body to the burying. Verily I say unto you, Wheresoever this gospel shall be preached throughout the whole world, this also that she hath done shall be spoken of for a memorial of her. (Mark 14:3-9.)

Concerns over the so-called waste of spikenard ointment on Jesus' head and Martha's anxiety over getting supper on the table illustrate how precious gospel perspective is. The meek may not always see at once, but they can be taught.

How fitting that the Lord of eternity should teach us so well the meaning of moments, for our lives, that "glide swiftly away": "The arrow is flown and the moments are gone."[5] How vital it is to be meek enough to choose the "good part": "But Martha was cumbered about much serving, and came to him, and said, Lord, dost thou not care that my sister hath left me to serve alone? bid her therefore that she help me. And Jesus answered and said unto her, Martha, Martha, thou art careful and troubled about many things: but one thing is needful: and Mary hath chosen that good part, which shall not be taken away from her." (Luke 10:40-42.)

The trailing commandment—endure well to the end—also requires meekness. What we are to do, we are to go on doing till the end of this life. In that setting, meekness is not surprised that the same afflictions found in the world are found in the Church, with fiery trials added thereto. (1 Peter 5:9; 4:12.) That which is expected is more easily endured. Though forewarned, the challenge is still there: "Beloved, seeing ye know these things before, beware lest ye also...fall from your own stedfastness." (2 Peter 3:17.)

President Spencer W. Kimball observed of a dimension of meekness that a person who is possessed of humility "seeks not to justify [his] follies." He further observed that "humility makes no bid for popularity or notoriety; demands no honors."[6]

If we do not have meekness, and do not feast upon the word of Christ to avoid weariness, the steady erosion of commitment proceeds. The cares of the world crowd even more. The very passage of time itself even creates its own form of weariness.

Seeing the unrighteous prosper and pleasure-seekers go unpunished can take its toll too, unless we are meek. So can the accumulation of afflictions and our awareness thereof. Such harrowing can create the fertile soil of self-pity with its "I deserve..." It is a surprisingly small step from weariness in well-doing to self-pity. The imagery of being grounded and rooted, of not being "moved away," warns us of that one small step that, when taken, nearly ensures a second. (See 1 Corinthians 15:58; Romans 2:7.)

So the risks are real that instead of holding fast, there will be a letting go which, once started, multiplies in its expressions like insects breeding in the sun. The unrooted are the first to go, enduring "but for a time." (Mark 4:17.) Thus, while the assurance that the Lord's grace is sufficient for the meek (Ether 12:26) does not mean an absence of adversity or a promise of repose and ease, it does bring inner strength and peace in the process of enduring all things. President Ezra Taft Benson observed that "humility does not mean weakness. It does not mean timidity. It does not mean fear. A man can be humble and fearless."[7]

Our lives can be in order though in tumult. The person who is never "weary of good works" (Alma 37:34) is yet able to rest. The promise of such is "peace in this world, and eternal life in the world to come." (D&C 59:23.) The meek individual can be unthreatened by the passage of time and unsurprised by either fiery trials or the events when "summer is nigh." This is the happy state of commandment keepers who "are blessed in all things." Still, they must "hold out faithful to the end." (Mosiah 2:41.) Such will, as Jesus declared, "find rest unto [their] souls." (Matthew 11:29.)

In contrast, those who are not meek refuse God's help, and, since He will compel no one into His kingdom, they need more help than can be justly given them. The apostle Peter observed how God "resisteth the proud, and giveth grace to the humble." (1 Peter 5:5.)

We can, if we are meek, "live in thanksgiving daily" (Alma 34:38), even while coping with our individualized curricula of life. Jesus taught, "If any man will come after me, let him deny himself, and take up his cross daily, and follow me." (Luke 9:23.) It is often the daily dimension of discipleship that is so difficult. We may rise to a crisis but fail amid routine.

Meekness and gratefulness for life amid the difficulties of each day will give us the attitude of thanksgiving, the very thing Alma prescribed. Doing this, however, requires an awareness in order to create appreciation of the "many mercies and blessings which [God] doth bestow." (Alma 34:38.) Awareness and appreciation can thus create a self-reinforcing attitude of thanksgiving, making these words a less stern requirement: "And whosoever doth not bear his cross, and come after me, cannot be my disciple." (Luke 14:27.) In Joseph Smith's rendering of this verse, these words have been added: "Wherefore, settle this in your hearts that ye will do the things which I shall teach and command you." (JST, Luke 14:28.) Meekness helps us to get things settled. Submissiveness to certain allotted circumstances cannot be achieved without the relevant meekness. Meekness not only brings its own rewards, it is also a virtue that, once in place and once our hearts are settled, can do much to renew itself.

Just how much the Lord is willing to put us through in order to attain and retain humility may be gauged by his relationship with ancient Israel, with whom He labored "forty years in the wilderness, to humble [them]." (Deuteronomy 8:2.)

Meekness is a quality bearing much upon our concluding status. Alma asked, if one were to die, could that person really say he or she had been "sufficiently humble"? (Alma 5:27.) The spiritual adornment of a particular people in the Book of Mormon was that they grew "stronger and stronger in their humility" as they increasingly yielded "their hearts unto God." (Helaman 3:35.)

Alma observed how "highly favored of the Lord" were those who had humbled themselves because of the words of the gospel preached to them by Helaman and his brethren. (Alma 48:19-20.)

Significantly, the coming forth of the Book of Mormon set forth in Isaiah and elsewhere in the scriptures was to be a glorious event, in connection with which the meek would "increase their joy in the Lord." (Isaiah 29:19. See also 2 Nephi 3:11.) But the proud will not take the book seriously. (2 Nephi 27:20.)

The love and patience necessary for long-suffering are not possible without meekness. Meekness knows no condescension. It does, however, know lamentation: "O Jerusalem, Jerusalem, ... how often would I have gathered thy children together, even as a hen gathereth her chickens under her wings, and ye would not!" (Matthew 23:37.)

Meekness does not rail at the realities of the universe, including the fact that, ultimately, blessings are dispensed according to obedience to the laws upon which they are based. We mortals are also free to choose—another reality that produces both felicity and misery.

The meek likewise understand another reality—that the Lord chastens those whom he loves, and, furthermore, that it is our faith and patience that are to be tried.

(Mosiah 23:21.) But our trials can occur in the context of precious perspective. "Thus God has provided a means that man, through faith, might work mighty miracles; therefore he becometh a great benefit to his fellow beings." (Mosiah 8:18.)

The meek are not offended, either, that the Church is for the perfecting of the saints; it is not a destination or a club limited only to those who are or who think they are perfect.

The unmeek may see consequences coming as a result of mistaken behavioral attitudes and yet do nothing. They are almost immobilized. On the other hand, the meek, as Peter observed, "see afar off." (2 Peter 1:9.) Yet in the midst of their being thus wise, they are also harmless; they strive for that kind of love about which the Apostle Paul wrote so movingly in the thirteenth chapter of First Corinthians.

The unmeek have a greater sense of deprivation because they have had higher expectations of life, whereas the meek are content with the things the Lord has allotted to them. (Alma 29:3.) Those who are not lowly but who have had high expectations often look for reasons for failure outside themselves. They are not wise and harmless but are often narrow and vengeful.

The lowly do not make high demands of life, though they have a high desire to serve. They are not drenched in an exaggerated sense of entitlement, but instead are drenched in gratitude over the marvelous basic blessings they have even in the midst of the disappointments of the day.

Jesus endured lesser spiritual maturity in the Twelve and in His other disciples. He endured this while helping to remedy it. He did this without condescension, without despairing, without cynicism, and without murmuring. We have only to look at His prayers to the Father for and in behalf of His disciples to see how perfect His love is.

(See John 17.) Indeed, when His followers deserved censure, they often received teaching. Though He spoke the truth to them, sometimes reprovingly, He spoke the truth in love. (Ephesians 4:15.)

It is both amazing and sobering to observe how the Father and the Son disclose vital truths to their sons and daughters, share with them, and tutor them. They are seeking to lift us up and to enhance us. They do all this without feeling diminished or threatened themselves. The more They tell us about their creations and their purposes, the more clearly we see the utter sincerity of that great redemptive declaration, "This is my work and my glory—to bring to pass the immortality and eternal life of man." (Moses 1:39.)

Thus the Father and the Son not only encourage emulation, but also promise rewards, as we draw closer to Them and become more like Them. Indeed, when we keep their commandments, They do "immediately bless" us. (Mosiah 2:24.) If we are willing and meek enough, we can become part of their community in which the Father will "share all that he hath" with us. (D&C 84:38.)

What a contrast to us mortals! At times we withhold time, talent, and knowledge from others in order to preserve a seeming advantage. Meanwhile, for those who have eyes to see and ears to hear, the Father and the Son, astonishingly, are giving away the secrets of the universe. If only we can avoid being offended by their generosity!

NOTES

1. *Interpreter's Dictionary of the Holy Bible*, p. 335.
2. Abraham Cannon Journal, April 9, 1890.
3. Ibid.
4. *Journal of Discourses* 9:125.
5. *Hymns*, 1985, no. 217.
6. Spencer W. Kimball, "Humility," *BYU Speeches of the Year*, January 1963.
7. Address at seminar for new mission presidents, June 22, 1979.

Chapter Seven

THE EXAMPLE OF
THE PROPHETS

"Blessed is he whosoever shall not be offended in me." (Matthew 11:6)

Jesus foresaw how and why He and His prophets would, in His mortal Messiahship, be rejected by so many. What He did, what He said, and what He was, offended many. The pattern is there, as well, with regard to the prophets sent by Jesus. The same meekness needed to accept Him is needed to accept His emissaries. Perhaps more is needed, the latter being good but imperfect. Without humbleness of mind, we are apt to reject those whom He has sent. There can be many excuses for rejecting the prophets. When meek enough, we know a prophet is a prophet. As President Brigham Young said of his predecessor: "He [the Lord] called upon his servant Joseph Smith, jun., when he was but a boy, to lay the foundation of his kingdom for the last time. Why did he call upon Joseph Smith to do it? because he was disposed to do it. Was Joseph Smith the only person on earth who could have done this work? No doubt there were many others who, under the direction of the Lord, could have done that work; but the Lord selected the one that pleased him, and that is sufficient."[1]

Yet the tendency to "unload" on Joseph Smith is growing in our day, reflecting the pattern of yesteryear. He was not long in the grave before some people began to make accusations about him. Of this President Young said, "They cannot let the dead alone, so great is their corruption and wickedness."[2]

When, by way of example, we ponder the Prophet Joseph Smith through the prisms of the past, we can see, among the factors at work, several that lent themselves to his being misrepresented, both then and now, causing some to be offended. Jesus is the premiere case, however.

To be sure, there are significant differences as to scale between the Lord and the very best of His servants. Nevertheless, the process has striking parallels between the Master and His servants who take His yoke upon them, as we see in the illustrations to follow.

First, Joseph Smith had an unusual amount of information foretelling what would befall him. This, for him at least, caused his future to impinge upon his present. There should be some allowance for this when the Prophet is viewed by worldly perspectives in any particular moment of his life.

Joseph's experience with regard to being misunderstood began early on with his first telling of his First Vision. This brought him persecution and caused him, as a basically trusting soul, to ponder about "how very strange it was," as he later wrote. He felt the stings of rejection, which became "the cause of great sorrow" to him. (JS-H 1:23.)

By 1842 in Nauvoo, however, it had all become second nature to him. Moreover, in the midst of his large tasks, his afflictions were seen by him as "a small thing." Indeed, it all had to be accepted by him as his "common lot." (D&C 127:2.)

Joseph knew not only of his impending martyrdom but also of the final outcome: "I shall triumph over all my enemies, for the Lord God hath spoken it," he declared. (D&C 127:2.) Joseph clearly understood the reassuring reality of these words which had come through him: "There is nothing that the Lord thy God shall take in his heart to do but what he will do it." (Abraham 3:17.)

These foretellings could have created in the Prophet a

spirit of careless pride or immobilized fatalism—yet they did not. His perspective instead made him reluctant to enter every fray and to respond each time there was a false rumor or accusation. His human indignation was real but episodic—not unlike, in its periodic expressions, the impulsiveness of Peter in cutting off the ear of the servant of the high priest. (Luke 22:50.)[3]

Finally, however, submissive Joseph went "like a lamb to the slaughter"—but only after his appointed work was completed.

Granted, Joseph Smith was periodically surprised and indignant concerning certain things, including distortions by critics. Once he complained about how some "had power to lead the minds of the ignorant and unwary and thereby attain such influence that when we approached their iniquities the devil gained great advantage."[4] However, whatever the actual battle of the moment, so far as the enemies of the Church were concerned, Joseph expected "a long and tremendous warfare."[5]

Second, in the midst of all these things, Joseph—like his colleague prophets—was so busy being a special witness for the Savior that he had little time to heed all of the false witness being borne about him. Joseph was usually more inclined to endure than explain himself, even though the drumbeat of dissent was at certain points almost unrelieved. In Nauvoo, in March 1842, for instance, while intensively engaged "day and evening" in translating the Book of Abraham, he said that he simply did not have time to attend to all his public duties.[6] His duties as a seer were more important than his ceremonial chores.

Joseph did not respond at times, of course, such as by issuing a summational disclaimer as from the temple stand in Nauvoo, saying, "I never told you I was perfect; but there is no error in the revelations which I have taught."[7]

Third, Joseph not only had unusual perspective, but he

also had unusual empathy. Looking back upon his busy, task-filled years, he said, near the end, "No man knows my history. I cannot tell it: I shall never undertake it. I don't blame any one for not believing my history. If I had not experienced what I have, I would not have believed it myself."[8] Even in his adversity, Joseph Smith had remarkable empathy for those lacking his perspective. Thus he even seemed to understand why others could not understand. He sensed, for instance, how discouraging things must have looked to his followers when he was in Liberty Jail and twelve thousand Latter-day Saints had been driven from Missouri into misery and hardship. "Zion shall yet live though she seemeth to be dead," he consoled and reassured.[9] Joseph's enlarged perspective about things may actually have been a deterrent to his reacting automatically and tactically; he saw things strategically.

Joseph's empathy extended even to those beyond his own time and circumstances. He actually saw his own prison sufferings as helping him "to understand the minds of the Ancients."[10] He was to experience certain things so that a linkage was felt with their afflictions, so that, he said, "in the day of judgment ... we may hold an even weight in the balances with them."[11] How else except out of such polishing experiences could Joseph take his rightful place, "crowned in the midst of the prophets of old"?[12]

Fourth, Joseph was also unusually trusting of others. He was often too slow to conclude that certain people were betraying him. His reluctance to recognize betrayal drew the comment from his biographer, Elder B. H. Roberts, that in his generosity, he sometimes had "a too great tenacity in friendship for men he had once taken into his confidence after they had been proven unworthy of that friendship."[13]

The betrayals of some in his inner circle brought

understandable indignation. On occasion, however, these also appeared to have caused him to be more wistful than resentful. Wilford Woodruff apparently had such an experience during the Kirtland period when Joseph met him and shook his hand and seemed to look scrutinizingly into his eyes. The Prophet then made the comment how glad he was to see Brother Woodruff: "I hardly know when I meet those who have been my brethren ... who of them are my friends. They have become so scarce."[14]

So it was that Joseph's perspective, his remarkable concentration upon laying the foundation of the great latter-day restoration, and his empathy for and his trust of others—all are prisms through which he and his history are to be viewed. Seeing him deepening his discipleship while striving and struggling under Jesus' yoke is impressive indeed. While they provided a tremendous advantage to him and were certainly necessary in the Lord's work, these factors appear to have operated at times in such a way as to create tactical disadvantages, including what we today might call public relations problems. Joseph was, after all, justifiably preoccupied with his task of rolling off the kingdom onto the backs of the Twelve. This task occupied much of his time early in 1844, in the period just before his martyrdom, and overrode other concerns because he was so anxiously engaged.

On one near-final occasion, when he had blessed and instructed the Twelve for two or three hours in the upper room of the store in Nauvoo, the Prophet apparently felt he had finally achieved the objective of rolling the burdens of the kingdom off his shoulders onto theirs. He said, "I feel as light as a cork. I feel that I am free."[15] He then paced the room almost in exhilaration. He once said to one of the Twelve, "The hosts of Satan will not be able to tear down the kingdom, as fast as you will be able to build it up."[16]

Thus, while he was anxiously engaged in putting

such fundamental things in place, and having been told early on by Moroni that his "name would be had for good and evil among all people" (JS-H 1:33), that "fools shall have [him] in derision, and hell shall rage against [him]" (D&C 122:1), Joseph's posture was not a fretful, anxious public relations posture. Gospel perspective can bring the meekness that a role requires even when that role is misunderstood.

Perhaps the momentary, tactical disadvantages and distortions experienced by Joseph, some of which have been perpetuated to this day, were part of the prophecy his father relayed in December 1834, when he gave Joseph a foretelling blessing: "Though the wicked mar him for a little season ... he shall roar in his strength [and] he shall stand before the Lord, having produced a hundred fold."[17] Wide acclaim for the Prophet Joseph needed to be forgone "for a little season."

The spiritually educated will understand and will make allowance for such things when they assess the Prophet. It is the meek disciple who ensures that another prophecy about Joseph continues to be fulfilled: "Thy people shall never be turned against thee by the testimony of traitors." (D&C 122:3.)

Parallels from another period of Christian history may be profitably pondered for some added perspective about how a yoke assumed can enlarge one's empathy and meekness. Bearers of truth are often the victims of partial truths. Partial truths can sometimes have such an influence as to make full falsehoods green with envy. For instance, how might certain episodes in Jesus' mortal ministry have been viewed by some who lived then? Many individuals, lacking discernment and perspective, engaged in "looking beyond the mark." (Jacob 4:14.)

Examples follow, illustrating somewhat speculatively how some commentary might have gone then and how partial understandings might have caused the neglect of critical data about the divinity of meek Jesus. The examples are, of course, from "commentators" contemporaneous with Him:

Commentator A: We understand that the followers of Jesus of Nazareth claim that, about thirty years ago, three wise men journeyed great distances from the East to see the newly born so-called Messiah. Years ago, three visitors from the East visited with King Herod, who directed them to Bethlehem, the supposed place of the Messiah's birth. These men were apparently so unimpressed with whatever they later found that they did not bother even to report back to the king, as he had requested. (Matthew 2:1–12.) Besides, the individual under discussion is one Jesus of Nazareth, not Jesus of Bethlehem. As is well known, the Messiah was not to come out of Galilee.[18]

Commentator B: The followers of this Jesus of Nazareth, a carpenter's son, include the common people who hear Him (Mark 12:37), but His followers are clearly not from among the leaders of our society; they are instead the "unlearned and ignorant men" (Acts 4:13). Some of them are merely displaced fishermen from Galilee, who speak with a noticeable Galilean accent. (Mark 14:70.) We ask simply, "Have any of the rulers or of the Pharisees believed on him?" (John 7:48.)[19]

Commentator C: The followers of the Nazarene claim that He raised a young man named Lazarus from the dead, causing a great stir. (John 11; 12:11.) Since then, Jesus' followers have even represented that Lazarus's life was in jeopardy. (John 12:10.) But his own chroniclers—Matthew, Mark, and Luke—do not even mention this supposed miracle in their writings about the Nazarene.[20]

Commentator D: Jesus could not hold many of His followers. Once He gathered them on a fairly large scale, but this was largely because He was feeding them fish and bread. However, very soon even many of these left

Him, deserted His cause, and "walked no more with him." (John 6:66.) People need not only bread for relief from hunger, but also political leadership. Instead, Jesus began to refer to Himself as the "bread of life." (John 6:35, 48.)

The final test of any leader, therefore, must rest upon His appeal to the people and reflect the support He receives from them. Pilate, the Roman procurator, a detached observer, gave the assembled throng a fair and clear choice between a murderer, Barabbas, and the Nazarene. The crowd preferred Barabbas! (John 18:40.) Had Jesus definitely been a man of the people, He would have been spared. Other like-pretenders have come and gone, too, such as Theudas and Judas of Galilee. (Acts 5:34–40.)

Commentator E: With regard to Jesus' crucifixion, it must be remembered that hundreds of people have been crucified. There is nothing special about that punishment under the Romans. But the followers of Jesus apparently stole His body and then tried to claim that He was resurrected after His crucifixion. However, the Roman soldiers who were at the garden tomb indicate that no such thing as the miracle of the resurrection took place. These sentries merely dozed, contrary to their instructions, and the Nazarene's body was whisked away by followers![21]

So much for a few illustrative examples from meridian days. Neglect of vital data, use of partial truths, plus "looking beyond the mark," can cruelly combine to blunt perspective and create, as it were, public relations problems. Meek and lowly Jesus understood in advance, while those who were unmeek looked "beyond the mark." So it was, in fulfillment of prophecy, that "they hated [Jesus] without a cause." (John 15:25.)

Religious history shows one other factor related to

the virtue of meekness. There are often those who resent the spiritual preeminence of another. The spiritually sophisticated will make allowance for this tendency in evaluating the criticisms of the prophets. Jesus, as always, is the classic case: "And the Pharisees also, who were covetous, heard all these things: and they derided him." (Luke 16:14.)

This same pattern of resentment was encountered anciently by Moses and also by Nephi. Since God must work through imperfect individuals, whomever He chooses and then pours truths, prophecies, and revelations through will surely be resented by some. The Prophet Joseph Smith recognized this and once made a special pleading: "Now, brethren, let me tell you, that it is my disposition to give and *forgive,* and to bear & to *forbear,* with all long suffering and patience, with the foibles, follies, weaknesses, & wickedness of my brethren and all the world of mankind; and my confidence and love toward you is not slackened, nor weakened. And now, if you should be called upon to bear with us a little in any of our weaknesses and follies, ... don't be offended."[22]

The same resentment with regard to Joseph Smith exists even today. The truly educated will nevertheless keep such special men and their messages in proper perspective.

So it is that the meekness factor is at the center of the unfolding of the spiritual core of human history, determining who are the misunderstood and who are the misunderstanders. Moreover, those who do not value the process of deepening their discipleship will not see it. They will miss the spiritual significance of what it means to take Jesus' yoke upon us.

Yet how else can we experience, in our small measure, what He passed through for us? Learning of Him cannot be merely intellectual and abstract; it must be experiential and personal—just as He received His learning concerning our sins, sicknesses, pains, and infirmities! (See Alma 7:11–12; 2 Nephi 9:21.)

We can be "yokefellows" only if we are willing to be tutored and if we are willing to submit.

NOTES

1. *Journal of Discourses* 11:253.
2. Ibid., p. 664.
3. For Peter, though we lack details, "signifying by what death he would glorify God," martyrdom was preceded by much adversity. In the end, martyred but meek Peter may have even experienced crucifixion on an inverted cross. (John 21:19; 2 Peter 1:14.)
4. Dean C. Jessee, *The Personal Writings of Joseph Smith,* p. 380.
5. *History of the Church* 5:141. It is sobering to contemplate the adversary's "order of battle" and that upon it he focuses his fire power in order to keep us from learning of Jesus. (Matthew 11:29.) Any gain in any sector, on the part of the Lord's army, is cause for gladness. These points, however, which feel the adversary's most sustained and massed assaults, are instructive for us to contemplate. Issues pertaining to families, temples, prophets, and scriptures are those real pressure points. For instance, the adversary is not shelling the Church's athletic program nor is he inciting complaints over the Christmas lights on Temple Square. However, hell still rages against what is taught in temples.
6. *History of the Church* 4:548–49.
7. *History of the Church* 6:367.
8. Ibid., p. 317.
9. Jessee, *Personal Writings of Joseph Smith,* p. 382.
10. Ibid., p. 387.
11. Ibid., p. 395.
12. *Hymns,* 1985, no. 27.
13. B. H. Roberts, *Comprehensive History of the Church* 2:358.
14. Mathias F. Cowley, *Wilford Woodruff,* p. 68.
15. Leonard J. Arrington, *Brigham Young: American Moses,* p. 110.
16. "Trial of Elder Rigdon," *Times and Seasons,* September 15, 1844, p. 651.
17. Father's blessing given in December 1834 by Joseph Smith, Sr.
18. As far as we now know, Jesus' critics never asked Him where He was born. Ironically, His being a Nazarene had also been prophesied, according to Matthew. "And he came and dwelt in a city called Nazareth: that it might be fulfilled which was spoken by the prophets, He shall be called a Nazarene." (Matthew 2:23.) However, this question and this prophecy were ignored by many. The result was that "others said, This is the Christ. But some said, Shall Christ come out of Galilee?" (John 7:41.) Some said Jesus was Elias, others that he was John the Baptist returned, or another of the prophets. (Matthew 16:13–14.)
19. Some of the establishment did believe: "Nevertheless among the chief rulers also many believed on him; but because of the Pharisees they did not confess him, lest they should be put out of the synagogue: for they loved the praise of men more than the praise of God." (John 12:42–52.) But such did not go public until later: "And the word of God increased; and the number of the disciples multiplied in Jerusalem greatly; and a great company of the priests were obedient to the faith." (Acts 6:7.)

20. A Cambridge scholar and Christian, Frederic W. Farrar, wrote: "We seem to trace in the Synoptists a special reticence about the family at Bethany.... There is, therefore, a distinct argument for the conjecture that when the earliest form of the Gospel of St. Matthew appeared, and when the memorials were collected which were used by the other two Synoptists, there may have been special reasons for not recording a miracle which would have brought into dangerous prominence a man who was still living, but of whom the Jews had distinctly sought to get rid as a witness of Christ's wonder-working power (John xii. 10). Even if this danger had ceased, it would have been obviously repulsive to the quiet family of Bethany to have been made the focus of an intense and irreverent curiosity, and to be questioned about those hidden things which none have ever revealed. Something, then, seems to have 'sealed the lips' of those Evangelists—an obstacle which had been long removed when St. John's Gospel first saw the light." (*The Life of Christ*, p. 511.)

21. These carefully preserved verses give us some perspective as to the pressures mounted and what actually happened:

"But the chief priests moved the people, that he should rather release Barabbas unto them." (Mark 15:11.)

"Now the next day, that followed the day of the preparation, the chief priests and Pharisees came together into Pilate, saying, Sir, we remember that that deceiver said, while he was yet alive, After three days I will rise again. Command therefore that the sepulchre be made sure until the third day, lest his disciples come by night, and steal him away, and say unto the people, He is risen from the dead: so the last error shall be worse than the first. Pilate said unto them, Ye have a watch: go your way, make it as sure as you can. So they went, and made the sepulchre sure, sealing the stone, and setting a watch." (Matthew 27:62-66.)

"Now when they were going, behold, some of the watch came in to the city, and shewed unto the chief priests all the things that were done. And when they were assembled with the elders, and had taken counsel, they gave large money unto the soldiers, saying, Say ye, his disciples came by night, and stole him away while we slept. And if this come to the governor's ears, we will persuade him, and secure you. So they took the money, and did as they were taught: and this saying is commonly reported among the Jews until this day." (Matthew 28:11-15.)

22. Jessee, *The Personal Writings of Joseph Smith*, p. 318.

EPILOGUE

Meekness, though lowly, has its own quiet majesty. The process of learning experientially about, of, and from Jesus is such that by being yoked to Him and His gospel, we are drawn closer to Him. Proximity only increases our meekness. This undertaking requires time and obedience—two things implicit in being yoked.

Obedience, among other things, provides us with a grace period. During this period, we go forward out of a sense of duty, doing what we should do before we have all the answers as to why. The full witness often does not come "until after the trial of [our] faith." (Ether 12:6.) President Lorenzo Snow once said to the Twelve of his day, "Every one of us who has not already had the experience must yet meet it of being tested in every place where we are weak."[1] Moroni said that for the meek and fearful, the Lord will "make weak things become strong unto them." (Ether 12:27.)

Even advance knowledge does not remove the need for being obedient. Jesus, as the Creator of this and other worlds and as Jehovah of the Old Testament, back beyond time, was the Meek Volunteer: "Here am I, send me," He said. (Abraham 3:27.) This statement was not a bid for power or status on Jesus' part. His response reflected resolution, since He knew intellectually, though not experientially and perfectly, what He would have to pass through later. "Send me," therefore, was a statement of ripe obedience in the face of considerable knowledge of the consequences of that obedience.

Jesus' obedience, then and later, facilitated His perfection, including perfecting the attribute of mercy. His mortal Messiahship permitted Him to experience personally the human condition and the difficulties of preaching His gospel. His "O Jerusalem" lamentation reflected what He had experienced already as a loving Jehovah, yet it was met by an audience of rejecting "scribes and Pharisees, hypocrites!" (Matthew 23:29, 37.)

In His mortal Messiahship, He who had sent so many prophets now faced all that they had faced—and much more: "And when the Jews heard these things they were angry with him; yea, even as with the prophets of old, whom they had cast out, and stoned, and slain; and they also sought his life, that they might take it away. But behold, I, Nephi, will show unto you that the *tender mercies of the Lord* are over all those whom he hath chosen, because of their faith, to make them mighty even unto the power of deliverance." (1 Nephi 1:20; italics added.)

The Lord teaches us much about Himself through His "tender mercies." He also teaches us much about that which we may become, as we confront, on our scale, the individual curricula of our lives. His most apt pupils, of course, are the men and women of God. In those instances of record, the Lord has displayed much gentleness and tenderness in His tutoring of such individuals. The pattern usually involves His disclosing more about Himself and about His work, thus expanding the horizons of the person being tutored. He is likewise reassuring and assigns that favored individual a portion of His work, including declaring the gospel, while making special promises. The pattern, though mercifully scaled, is there in the lives of all true disciples.

Puzzled Enoch felt so inadequate when he was called. He asked the Lord, "Why is it that I have found favor in

MEEK AND LOWLY

thy sight, and am but a lad, and all the people hate me; for I am slow of speech; wherefore am I thy servant?" The Lord reassured Enoch, but only by addressing him as "my son." (Moses 6:31, 27.) Enoch, with later and greater perspective, grew lovingly anxious—not over himself but over the Lord's work, wondering why God weeps and when the earth will rest. (Moses 7:29, 58, 63-64.) Enoch wept too as his heart "swelled wide as eternity." (Moses 7:41.) He pled mercifully for blessings upon the children of Noah. (Moses 7:49.)

We see the same pattern of tutorial tenderness and the same divine disclosure with Abraham: "Thus I, Abraham, talked with the Lord, face to face, as one man talketh with another; and he told me of the works which his hands had made; and he said unto me: My son, my son (and his hand was stretched out), behold I will show you all these. And he put his hand upon mine eyes, and I saw those things which his hands had made, which were many; and they multiplied before mine eyes, and I could not see the end thereof." (Abraham 3:11-12.)

Once again, it is noteworthy how the outreaching Lord addressed Abraham as "my son, my son" and how Abraham was given such stunning promises.

The same pattern is there with regard to the prophet Moses, whom the Lord also repeatedly addressed "my son." Having called Moses to deliver His people from bondage, the Lord shared and disclosed the workmanship of His hands on this planet, showing Moses many lands with inhabitants "numberless as the sand upon the sea shore." He called Moses to perform a work even as He expanded Moses' horizon by displaying some of His handiwork. Though overwhelmed, Moses, with presence of mind, asked the creating Lord why these things were so, evoking the spectacular summation of Divine intent: "For behold, this is my work and my glory—to bring to pass the immortality and eternal life of man." (Moses 1.)

It was doubtless much the same later, when Paul was

116

attended to by the resurrected Jesus who had come to cheer the apostle while Paul was in prison one night. (Acts 23:11.) We do not have the dialogue from that occasion, but it included Paul's being commended for declaring Jesus' gospel and testifying of the Lord in Jerusalem—and now Paul was called to labor in Rome.

The pattern prevailed with Joseph Smith, including while he was in Liberty Jail. The Lord referred to Joseph as "my son," and gave startling and marvelous reassurances along with a pointed but tender reminder of the comparative weight of pressing yokes: "The Son of Man hath descended below them all. Art thou greater than he?" (D&C 121, 122.)

In each of these instances, the more the Lord shared His perspective with these outstanding individuals, the more anxious they were to become like Him and to assist Him with His work. The more they came to know of the Lord and the closer they became to Him, the more tender and expansive His tutorials. Alas, for most people it is otherwise: "For how knoweth a man the master whom he has not served, and who is a stranger unto him, and is far from the thoughts and intents of his heart?" (Mosiah 5:13.)

For serious disciples, the greater their knowledge, the greater their meekness. The more such individuals associate with and are taught by the Lord, the more they strive to become like Him and the more they wish to declare His gospel. They rejoice exceedingly when the message is heeded, like the outreaching sons of Mosiah: "Now they were desirous that salvation should be declared to every creature, for they could not bear that any human soul should perish; yea, even the very thoughts that any soul should endure endless torment did cause them to quake and tremble." (Mosiah 28:3.) As Joseph Smith taught, either we are "drawing towards God" or "drawing towards the devil."[2]

Regarding divine tutorials, we must not overlook

ancient Joseph who was sold into Egypt, though the record we have of him is far from complete. His closeness to the Lord ensured that he was tutored. (See 2 Nephi, chapter 3, as an example.) Specifically, by way of example, when Joseph Smith, Sr., gave his prophet son a father's blessing in December 1834, he quoted extensively and directly from ancient Joseph. Ancient Joseph, who was anxious about his posterity, wept when he saw what would befall them as he learned that one of his own seed would be the means of bringing the gospel to his posterity in the latter days, and he rejoiced! Again, the tender phrase, "my son," appeared along with the salvational surge that flows through men and women of God with regard to their desire to see their family, their posterity, and all mankind enjoy the blessings of the gospel. The prophet Lehi became most desirous that his family "should partake of it also," referring to the fruit of the tree of life. (1 Nephi 8:12.)

These patterns of gentleness and tenderness are too striking to be accidental. They are even reflected in the voice of the Lord in its timbre and demeanor; it is pleasant and gentle, "a still voice of perfect mildness, as if . . . a whisper." To the Nephites, "it did pierce them that did hear to the center, insomuch that there was no part of their frame that it did not cause to quake; yea, it did pierce them to the very soul, and did cause their hearts to burn." (3 Nephi 11:3.)

Even the Lord's angelic messengers reflect His tenderness, as in this instance wherein an angel revisited, reassured, instructed, and commended diligent Alma: "Blessed art thou, Alma; therefore, lift up thy head and rejoice, for thou hast great cause to rejoice; for thou hast been faithful in keeping the commandments of God from the time which thou receivedst thy first message from him. Behold, I am he that delivered it unto you." (Alma 8:15.)

The stunning episode atop the Mount of Transfiguration doubtless involved the same pattern of disclosing, calling, reassuring, instructing, and blessing with regard to Peter, James, and John. Though we do not have all of the unspeakable particulars of what occurred there, those disciples received special blessings and insights as a result of being there. (Matthew 17:1–9.) But they would not have been on the spiritual height had they not been sufficiently lowly.

In any case, we see that the pattern of blessing, expanding, reassuring, calling, and endowing is reflective of the generosity as well as the gentleness of our Father, God, and His Son, Jesus Christ.

The words of Elder James E. Talmage part a curtain that opens to our view another possibility as to what the yoke required of Jesus: "It seems that, in addition to the fearful suffering incident to crucifixion, the agony of Gethsemane had recurred, intensified beyond human power to endure. In that most bitter hour, the dying Christ was alone, alone in most terrible reality. That the supreme sacrifice of the Son might be consummated in all of its fulness, the Father seems to have withdrawn the support of His immediate Presence, leaving to the Savior of men the glory of complete victory over the forces of sin and death."[3]

Some of us may likewise experience, on our scale of action, brief aloneness in adversity. This condition of severe mercy will obtain in order that we might have, as did Jesus, complete victory. Surely this is one of the ultimate dimensions of taking His yoke upon us so that we might learn of Him.

In multiple scriptural references, Jesus is described as having trod the winepress alone. In fact, the very symbolism of the red-colored garment that Jesus will apparently wear in one of His appearances at the time of His majestic second coming will be a reminder of how,

drenched in blood, He once trod the winepress alone.
(Genesis 49:11; Isaiah 63:3; Revelation 19:13; D&C 76:107.)
The aloneness spoken of does not imply abandonment,
but instead, that tutorial mercy in which a merciful
Father desired His Son's triumph to be complete. No
mortal was excluded from the tender mercies of the
Atonement because of the completeness of Christ—
which completeness reflected His meekness.

If we would be with Them, whether on mountaintop
or forever, we should ponder anew these sobering
words: "For none is acceptable before God, save the
meek and lowly in heart." (Moroni 7:44.)

NOTES

1. Abraham H. Cannon Journal, April 9, 1890.
2. *History of the Church* 4:588.
3. James E. Talmage, *Jesus the Christ*, p. 661.

BIBLIOGRAPHY

Arrington, Leonard J. *Brigham Young, American Moses*. New York: Alfred A. Knopf, 1985.

Church News section of the *Deseret News* (Salt Lake City, Utah).

Colville, John. *The Fringes of Power*. New York: Hodder and Stoughton Ltd., 1985.

Cowley, Matthias F. *Wilford Woodruff*. Salt Lake City: Deseret News, 1909.

Ehat, Andrew F., and Lyndon W. Cook, comps. *The Words of Joseph Smith*. Provo: Brigham Young University, 1980.

Farrar, Frederic W. *The Life of Christ*. London: Cassell, Petter & Galpin.

Fairlie, Henry. *The Seven Deadly Sins Today*. London: University of Notre Dame Press, 1979.

Great Books. Aquinas I & II.

Harrington, Michael. *The Politics at God's Funeral*. New York: Holt, Rinehart and Winston, 1983.

Hayward, Alan. *God Is*. Nashville: Thomas Nelson, Inc., 1980.

Interpreter's Dictionary of the Bible. Nashville: Abingdon Press, 1962.

James, Robert Rhodes, ed. *Churchill Speaks*. Leicester, England: Chelsea House Publishers, 1980.

Jessee, Dean C., ed. *The Personal Writings of Joseph Smith*. Salt Lake City: Deseret Book, 1984.

Journal of Discourses. 26 vols. London: Latter-day Saints Book Depot, 1854-1886.

Kimball, Spencer W. "Humility." *Speeches of the Year, 1963*. Provo: Brigham Young University.

Lee, Harold B. *Stand Ye in Holy Places*. Salt Lake City: Deseret Book, 1974.

Lewis, C. S. *The Last Battle*. New York: The Macmillan Company, 1956.

Longford, Elizabeth. *Wellington: Pillar of State*. St. Alban's, England: Granada Publishing Ltd., 1975.

————. *Wellington: The Years of the Sword.* St. Alban's, England: Granada Publishing Ltd., 1976.

MacDonald, George. *Life Essential.* Wheaton, Illinois: Harold Shaw Publishers, 1974.

McDowell, Bart. *The Revolutionary War.* Washington, D.C.: The National Geographic Society, 1967.

Morgan, Ted. *Churchill: Young Man in a Hurry, 1874-1915.* New York: Simon and Schuster, 1982.

Roberts, Brigham H. *A Comprehensive History of the Church of Jesus Christ of Latter-day Saints.* 6 vols. plus index. Salt Lake City: Deseret Book.

Smith, Joseph. *History of the Church of Jesus Christ of Latter-day Saints.* 7 vols. plus index. Salt Lake City: Deseret Book.

————. *Lectures on Faith.* Salt Lake City: Deseret Book, 1985.

Smith, Joseph Fielding, comp. *Teachings of the Prophet Joseph Smith.* Salt Lake City: Deseret Book, 1976.

Talmage, James E. *Jesus the Christ.* Salt Lake City: Deseret Book, 1974.

Times and Seasons (Nauvoo, Illinois). 1839-1846.

Tuchman, Barbara W. *The March of Folly.* New York: Alfred A. Knopf, 1984.

INDEX

Enoch, 115-16
Esteem for fellowman, 86
Exclusivism and pride, 63
Existence, premortal, 42

Fairlie, Henry, on pride, 51
Faith, 28-29, 48, 84
Fall, as result of pride, 53
Fellowman, esteem for, 86
Form vs. force, 18
Founding Fathers, 20, 26
Free agency, 42-43, 90-91

Gentleness of God, 115-20
Gladness, gospel, 39-40, 46
God: is source of power, 9;
    preoccupation of, 12; cares
    for his church, 14-15;
    tenderness of, 44; nature of,
    70-71; timetable of, 89-92; will
    of, 93; love of, 101-2; mercy
    of, 115-20
Gospels, 113 n. 20
Grace of God, 67, 98
Graciousness, 8-9, 94
Gratefulness, 99, 101
"Great question." See Question
Grumpiness, 57

Happiness, meekness is vital
    for, 16
Hardheartedness, 93
Harrison, R. K., quotation from,
    82 n.
Hayward, Alan, quotations
    from, 29-30, 59
Hobbies among Church
    members, danger of, 63
Holy Ghost, 40; testifies, 43
Hotel, African, 30
Humility. See Meekness

Inheritance of the earth, 95-96
Integrity of Jesus, 11

Intelligence, 36-37
Intellect: and meekness, 34,
    37-38, 41, 47; and
    stubbornness, 68
Israelites, disobedience of,
    15-16, 28-29; "holy people,"
    62
"It mattereth not," 32 n.

James and John, mother of, 10
Jehovah-Jesus, 35
Jeremiah, 88
Jesus Christ: yoke of, 1-3, 5,
    12-13, 16, 119; great question
    regarding, 2-3, 12, 37;
    atonement of, 7, 14, 119-20;
    meekness of, 7-8, 84; Bread
    of Life, 8; graciousness of, 8-9;
    integrity of, 11; possessions
    of, 11; watches over His
    church, 14; leadership of, 17,
    32; and Moses, 35; intellectual
    meekness of, 38-39;
    submissiveness of, 39;
    rejoiced, 45; in America,
    44-45; reproves those who
    murmur, 61; called Israelites
    "holy people," 62; disciples
    of, 67; introduces self to
    Nephites, 70; on failure to
    come to Him, 71-72;
    gentleness of, 84; timetable
    of, 89; enlarged view of,
    96-97; love of, 101-2;
    contemporary accounts of,
    108-10; crucifixion of, 110;
    was Nazarene, 112 n. 18;
    obedience of, 114-15; voice
    of, 118
Jonah, 55
Joseph of Egypt, 94-95, 118
Joy, 45-46. See also Gospel
    Gladness
Judas, 11, 95